HOW
SHALL
WE DIE
?

To

Ray Geis and Linda Geis,

two physicians who care,

and

Sally Bauman Harrison,

for a lifetime of caring

HOW SHALL WE DIE

Helping Christians Debate Assisted Suicide

EDITED BY
SALLY B. GEIS &
DONALD E. MESSER

ABINGDON PRESS/ Nashville

How Shall We Die?:
Helping Christians Debate Assisted Suicide

This book is printed on recycled, acid-free paper.

Library of Congress Cataloging-in-Publication Data

How shall we die? :   helping Christians debate assisted suicide-/
-edited by Sally B. Geis & Donald E. Messer.
   p.   cm.
Includes bibliographical references and index.
ISBN 0-687-06140-7 (alk. paper)
  1. Assisted suicide—Religious aspects—Christianity.
2. Euthanasia—Religious aspects—Christianity.   3. Right to die—
Religious aspects—Christianity.   I. Geis, Sally B., 1928– .
II. Messer, Donald E.
R726.H68   1997
179.7—dc21   96-53439

Scripture quotations are taken from the New Revised Standard Version Bible, Copyright 1989 by the Division of Christian Education of the National Council of the Churches of Christ in the USA. Used by permission.

The Appendix is taken from *Deciding About Life's End: A United Methodist Resource Book About Advance Directive*, Copyright © 1994 Health and Welfare Ministries Program Department, General Board of Global Ministries, The United Methodist Church, and is used by permission.

The excerpt on p. 28 from *How Could I Not Be Among You?* by Ted Rosenthal is Copyright © 1973 by Ted Rosenthal. Reprinted by permission of Persea Books, Inc.

97 98 99 00 01 02 03 04 05 06 — 10 9 8 7 6 5 4 3 2 1

MANUFACTURED IN THE UNITED STATES OF AMERICA

CONTENTS

ACKNOWLEDGMENTS

Thinking and talking about death, unfortunately, is"verboten" among many friends and families, not to mention the church and greater society. So to speak openly about suicide, euthanasia, and assisted suicide certainly is to break the barrier.

Yet few issues are more urgent in the church and society today than a serious debate and dialogue about these matters. The personal and social stakes are too high for such concerns to be simply left to the professionals and politicians. Thus this study book invites readers at all ages and stages in life to participate in the deliberations and decisions.

Collaborating on a book-writing project of this nature requires the deepest of friendships among the editors, since a multitude of decisions must be made about the choice of topics, authors, style, time-line, and so on. If we did not share a multitude of reciprocal interests and commitments, understanding might run thin when disagreements occur or approaches differ. Instead, the experience of writing only deepens our mutual respect and enhances our joy at being able to work together.

This book is the second in a series of volumes designed to help Christians of differing theological and ethical perspectives confront contemporary personal and social issues. *Caught in the Crossfire: Helping Christians Debate Homosexuality* (Abingdon Press, 1994) brought together, for the first time, conservative and liberal Christians in honest and open dialogue about the same questions. Readers have found it beneficial not only in terms of understanding homosexuality, but also in comprehending why sisters and brothers of the faith can differ so radically on this subject.

Likewise, this study book aims to clarify differences and broaden understandings as to why Christians differ so sharply on questions related to the termination of life, suicide, and assisted suicide. We are greatly indebted to the diverse Roman Catholic and Protestant (both evangelical and mainline) authors who contributed essays. Their timely and thoughtful responses to the case studies will enable others to think through the vital issues at stake for all concerned.

Working together at The Iliff School of Theology, we are privileged to have great support from the Board of Trustees, our academic colleagues, and administrative staff. In particular, we want to underscore our gratitude to Revel Loedy, Alberta Smith, Paul Millette, and Suzanne Calvin, as well as Maggie Roe, our student assistant. Others offering advice and assistance were Ann Luke, Margaret Hoeppner, Isabel D. Lopez, and Bob Olmstead. We deeply appreciate the critical reviews of the manuscript by Bonnie J. Messer, Christine M. Gallagher, Paul Murphy, Harvey C. Martz, Paul J. Kottke, and Delwin and Nancy Brown. Special thanks are extended to Ruth L. Fuller, M.D., and J. Raymond Geis, M.D., who offered counsel about the case studies.

None of these persons, of course, bears responsibility for the final text, but we know that without their generous contributions and assistance, the quality of this book would have suffered significantly. Thus to all who encouraged and assisted us, from the depths of our hearts we echo the words of William Shakespeare: "I can no other answer make but thanks, and thanks, and ever thanks."

CONTRIBUTORS

Lisa Sowle Cahill, Professor of Theology at Boston College, is President of the Society of Christian Ethics. She has served as visiting scholar at the Kennedy Institute of Ethics, Georgetown University, and as President of the Catholic Theological Society of America. She is the author of several books and serves on the editorial board of a number of scholarly journals, including *The Journal of Medicine and Philosophy.* She is a contributor to the *Encyclopedia of Bioethics.*

Nigel M. de S. Cameron is Provost as well as Professor of Theology and Culture at Trinity International University. Dr. Cameron is a Contributing Editor to *Christianity Today,* and until recently was editor of the journal *Ethics and Medicine.* He has written and edited a number of books. *The New Medicine: Life and Death After Hippocrates* is the most recent.

John B. Cobb, Jr. is Emeritus Professor of Theology and Co-Director of the Center for Process Studies, School of Theology at Claremont. He has coedited eight books and written more than two dozen. Most relevant to this topic is *Matters of Life and Death,* published in 1991. His latest publications include *Sustaining the Common Good* and *Grace and Responsibility: A Wesleyan Theology for Today.*

Mark A. Duntley, Jr. is ordained in the Presbyterian Church, USA, and serves as Chaplain and Assistant Professor of Religious Studies at Lewis and Clark College. His articles have appeared in *Sojourners* and *The Christian Century.* His frequent lectures on medical ethics include such topics as euthanasia, physician-assisted suicide, duties of HIV-infected health-care professionals, and reproductive autonomy & responsibility.

Sally B. Geis, founding director of the Iliff Institute for Lay and Clergy Education, holds a clinical faculty appointment in the Department of Psychiatry at the University of Colorado Health Sciences Center. She is a contributor to journals such as *The Journal of Family Practice* and *Death Studies.* She coedited two books with Donald E. Messer and was a member of the committee that developed the official United Methodist statement on death and dying.

Bruce Hilton, a full-time consultant, teacher, and writer in bioethics since 1971, is director of the National Center for Bioethics in Sacramento, California, and a member of four hospital ethics committees. A United Methodist clergyman, he writes a syndicated bioethics column for the Scripps-Howard News Service, and is author of five books, including *First, Do No Harm: Wrestling with the New Medicine's Life-and-Death Dilemmas.*

Joretta L. Marshall is an ordained United Methodist clergywoman, currently serving on the faculty at Iliff School of Theology in Denver, Colorado, where she teaches in the area of pastoral theology, care and counseling. Dr. Marshall previously served on the faculty at Vanderbilt Divinity School as a college chaplain and as a member of a pastoral team for a local church. She is the author of numerous articles and two books, soon to be published.

Richard A. McCormick, S.J., John A. O'Brien Professor of Christian Ethics, University of Notre Dame, previously served as Rose F. Kennedy Professor of Christian Ethics at the Kennedy Institute of Ethics, Georgetown University. His fifteen books include *Health and Medicine in the Catholic Tradition.* He is a frequent contributor to journals such as the *Hastings Center Report, Journal of Medicine and Philosophy,* and *Journal of the American Medical Association.*

Donald E. Messer, President of Iliff School of Theology, is Henry White Warren Professor of Practical Theology. His eight books include *Contemporary Images of Christian Ministry* and *A Conspiracy of Goodness.* He is coeditor of two recent volumes: *Caught in the Crossfire: Helping Christians Debate Homosexuality* with Sally B. Geis, and *Unity, Liberty, and Charity: Building Bridges Under Icy Waters,* with William J. Abraham.

Cornish R. Rogers, Associate Dean and the E. Stanley Jones Professor of Evangelism, Ecumenics, and Mission at the School of Theology in Claremont, was also the founding Director of the Urban Ministries Study program. He is a contributing editor of *Christian Century* and was recently featured in a videotape series on the "Letter to the Hebrews," produced by The United Methodist Publishing House. He is coeditor of a book on preaching from the Book of Revelation, *Preaching Through the Apocalypse.*

Robert M. Veatch is Director of The Kennedy Institute of Ethics, Georgetown University. He also has served as Staff Director, Research Group on Ethics and Health Policy, The Hastings Center. Author and editor of a score of books in the field of medical ethics, including *Death, Dying, and the Biological Revolution,* he serves on the editorial board of numerous scholarly journals and is associate editor of the *Encyclopedia of Bioethics.* His most recent publication is *Ethical Issues in Death and Dying,* edited with Tom L. Beauchamp.

J. Philip Wogaman is Senior Minister of Foundry United Methodist Church in Washington, D.C. Prior to his current appointment, he was Professor of Christian Ethics at Wesley Theological Seminary in Washington. He is the author of fifteen books, including *Christian Ethics: A Historical Introduction* and *Christian Moral Judgment.* He also writes *Wogaman Commentaries,* an online ethical commentary for The United Methodist News Service.

CHAPTER ONE

INTRODUCTION
A Time to Die

Sally B. Geis

T here are so many new books about dying that there are now special shelves set aside for them in book shops, along with the health-diet and home-repair paperbacks and the sex manuals. Some of these are so packed with detailed information and step-by-step instructions for performing the function that you'd think this was a new sort of skill which all of us are now required to learn. The strongest impression the casual reader gets, leafing through, is that proper dying has become an extraordinary, even an exotic experience, something only the specially trained get to do."[1]

This quotation opens Lewis Thomas' essay, "On Natural Death." For me, it has special significance because a dear friend and mentor sent it to me when he learned that I was giving a lecture titled, "How Shall We Die?" How gently this ninety-year-old Episcopal priest cautioned the use of humility when discussing death.[2] Perhaps he feared I would assume more wisdom about this mystery than, in fact, I possess. So it is with trepidation that I participate in the creation of yet another book about dying. Readers should proceed with the same caution my friend suggested to me. Remember, there have never been any follow-up studies to confirm that any "how to" advice was actually helpful to those who have completed life's journey.

In light of such misgivings, what factors persuaded my co-editor and me to offer this commentary about appropriate death? First of all, we write for a specific audience—women and men who take their Christian faith seriously and strive to live and die, as far as they are able, in an appropriate manner as dictated by their religious tradition. We believe these persons are in urgent need of theological and ethical resources that will help them resolve the dilemmas that surround death in this hi-tech medical, western world at the beginning of the twenty-first century.

Any satisfying answer to these difficult questions requires a theological, as well as a legal, medical, economic, and psychosocial discussion. Decades ago, sociologist William Ogburn advanced the theory of cultural lag.[3] By this he meant that the material or technological features of a society usually change more rapidly than do the norms, beliefs, values, and patterns of social organization. This produces stress on members of the society until they are able to readjust these patterns to accommodate the technological changes. Today increasing numbers of patients, families, and health-care providers are being victimized by a form of cultural lag. They are caught in the dilemma of prolonged death created by "advances" in medicine. They lack an adequate set of beliefs and a pattern of social organization that will help them negotiate the events that surround these newly created prolonged-death circumstances.

Most persons we know are anxious to "do the right thing," but how are they to know right from wrong when medical technology can keep patients alive almost indefinitely? Is it moral to watch a loved one suffer inordinately while waiting for the end? Should faithful Christians hold fast to the rules of the past, or should they participate in a revision of the old proscriptions in light of changed circumstances?

In spite of the urgent need for answers, many religious leaders tend to avoid the issue. Reasons for such avoidance are numerous and understandable. Many clergy are as uncomfortable with the new circumstances as are others in society. Furthermore, some clergy may actually have been taught in seminary that they should not "give advice" on these matters, that this sort of decision is so personal that it should be devoid of influence by outsiders, including the clergy. Other factors, including lack of information, theological uncertainty, or personal anxiety and fear also may inhibit clergy.

We offer this book to clergy and laity alike. Our intent is to give patients, family members, health-care professionals, and other caretakers permission to ask questions about life-terminating decisions, questions heretofore often forbidden within the Christian community. Or, as a young physician said when I asked him what the major goal should be, "Tell them it's OK to ask blunt questions, such as, 'Will you help me die?' " We believe that only through honest, thoughtful dialogue among those involved in decision-making, can our norms, values, and patterns of social organization be reformulated or reappropriated in ways that honor the integrity of our Christian tradition.

We Speak of Assisted Death with One Heart, but Many Minds

Each chapter, 2 through 6, begins with a short description of a real situation, within which a person or persons experienced death. Each case study was selected to illustrate one of the life-terminating options currently being earnestly debated within religious and medical communities. The case studies describe a variety of circumstances in which patients seek to control the time of their death. In some situations, the dying individual is assisted in this effort by a significant person in his or her life—physician, son, friend, or spouse. The description of the circumstances surrounding each death is followed by commentaries written from differing perspectives on the moral appropriateness of the actions taken by the patient, family, or physician in the case.

Life-terminating measures utilized in the case studies progress from the least to the most invasive measures currently available. The first commentary describes an elderly man who refused all treatment for cancer; the next tells of a young man who wanted the treatment he was receiving withdrawn. In the following one, a young woman is assisted by her physician, who prescribes a lethal dose of medication. She wanted to end her life because its quality had diminished due to her irreversible symptoms. Next we read of an elderly man who asked his son to help him end his suffering. They placed a plastic sack over the father's head after sedating medication had been administered. The final story is of an elderly couple who jointly committed suicide.

Each chapter ends with a short summary, followed by discussion questions which can be used while reading alone or in community. We confess a preference for community discussion because we believe that collective judgment about normative issues is often preferable to individual judgment made in isolation. By community, we mean a group of persons who represent a variety of perspectives that could inform and influence individual decision-making. Family members who have attended the death of a loved one should be included, as well as patients themselves. Group dialogue will benefit from the inclusion of health-care providers, authorities in the law, economists, social workers, psychologists— to name only a few whose professional interests may be involved with issues related to death.

Chapter 7, "When It's My Turn, How Will I Decide?" suggests a theological/ethical framework by which a concerned Christian might make a responsible decision about life-terminating procedures. However, we, the editors, have no intention of prescribing a specific, absolute answer to every Christian's circumstances. Each of us is called to make our own prayerful decision, in consultation with clergy, family, and friends. Some readers may find it helpful to read Chapter 7 first. It may assist one in gaining clarity about a possible theoretical framework for decision-making before the case-study chapters are read.

A short annotated bibliography appears near the end of the book, designed for individuals and study groups who seek practical, readable materials about dying with dignity. Finally, an appendix of sample documents illustrates some possible options for making one's end-of-life wishes known. Limitations of both the bibliography and the case studies should be noted. There is no discussion of a number of important death-related situations, including some of the common causes of prolonged dying—for example, a patient who has suffered a stroke or congestive heart failure. We do not address sudden or violent death, such as youth suicide, the death of children, persons in coma, or others unable to speak for themselves. Nor have we reviewed the growing body of literature related to hospice care, grief, and bereavement. All of these are important topics, omitted due to limitations of space, rather than a lack of concern.

The rationale for using true stories to initiate a theological and ethical discussion about life-terminating decisions was chosen because of the editors' experiences as ethicist and clergy at the bedside of the dying (Messer) and as a hospice consultant and staff member working with patients and families dealing with terminal illness (Geis). We believe those faced with life-and-death decisions for themselves or loved ones yearn for answers. Unfortunately, no definitive answers are forthcoming. Ultimately, death's arrival remains shrouded in mystery, despite our best efforts to deal with it rationally. Learning about the experience of others is often more helpful than academic discussions of abstract principles alone.

Death Decisions Are Unique and Irreversible, Never Totally Predictable or Controllable

A wise psychiatrist who consults in oncology wards is fond of reminding staff members who work with patients in end-of-life situations that *dying is a process, not a single act.* For this devout Presbyterian psychiatrist, who has seen patients for more than three decades, there is no such thing as a "generic death" that can be isolated and spoken of in absolute and abstract terms. She contends that death begins when an individual is born. It is not a static event at the end of life. Each human life and death is the result of a complex variety of psychological, spiritual, and cultural factors. Born poor and black herself, she often reminds her white, middle-class staff about factors that matter—race (African American mortality rates are significantly higher than Anglo rates), and socioeconomic class (which determines one's access to medical care).[4]

Psychologist Jeanette Modrick reminds us that gender is an important factor, too:

> Women are generally the caretakers for the terminally ill, caring for children, spouses and parents. . . . Women themselves often outlive their spouses and die alone. . . . Women's terminal illnesses are often not well understood, as health-care research has primarily been done on male patients. . . . Women are less likely to have their wishes in dying honored, as they are perceived as not knowing what they want (in the absence of a living will, men's previously expressed preferences regarding withdrawal of treatment are honored 75% of the time by the courts, while women's preferences are honored only 14% of the time).[5]

Religious heritage, family structure, and community relationships are also critical variables that influence decisions about living and dying. Each death, moreover, is unique because the course of each illness is unique. The amount of pain, the likelihood of irreversible depression, the quality of family support, the extent of economic resources—all vary case by case. Death, like life, is never totally predictable or controllable.

Decisions about how to die are usually made under less than ideal circumstances, in which virtually every choice involves some pain or distress. Ultimately, the abstract theoretical analyses of concepts, such as passive and active euthanasia or suicide and assisted suicide, must be applied to a specific life situation. Human reality and moral considerations must be joined, and an *irreversible* decision made about the future of an individual, within the context of her or his relationships.

It is useful to remember that traditional moral assumptions about assisting the dying to end their lives were never as clear-cut as some assume. Most health-care providers and family members who face terminal illnesses are lay Christians, not schooled in the nuances of ethical and theological discourse. They always have been faced with a measure of confusion as they try to understand what religion says about assisted suicide. Two significant examples make the point:

1. Definitions

Ethical literature identifies two types of life-terminating action that may be taken by a caretaker. Active euthanasia is action that *causes* physical death—for example, administration of an overdose of medication. This action infers legal as well as moral culpability. Passive euthanasia is action that *allows* another person to die—for example, by withholding life-support systems. Passive euthanasia is judged by most to suggest neither moral nor legal culpability. Anyone who has worked in a hospice knows that sometimes the line between active and passive euthanasia is less clear-cut than the analytical literature would lead one to believe. How is the nurse or physician to know *exactly* when a dose of medication strong enough to control pain will suppress the breathing of an already weak and dying patient? The guideposts meant to offer clear directions about death-related behavior are often unclear or contradictory, because life, and death itself, is often paradoxical.

2. Moral Teachings

As Christians, most of us learned certain biblical rules by which we try to live. One of the Ten Commandments says, "You shall not kill" (Exodus 20:13). However, the plight of some terminally ill loved ones who suffer with pain and diminishment that cannot be reversed leads us also to think deeply about the Golden Rule: "Do unto others as you would have others do to you" (Matthew 7:12). We ask ourselves, "If I were suffering this much, might I not ask for help to bring the suffering to an end? If I might want this for myself, what am I to do if my loved one asks me to help?"

Those on both sides of the debate about the legitimacy of assistance in dying quote the moral tenet, "Christians believe in the sanctity of life." But this statement is open to differing interpretations. One understanding suggests that if life is sacred, it must be preserved at any cost. Dietrich Bonhoeffer said, "In the sight of God, there is no life that is not worth living; for life itself is valued by God."[6] But another great theologian, Reinhold Niebuhr, said, "For the ending of our life would not threaten us if we had not falsely made ourselves the center of life's meaning."[7] How is the well-meaning layperson to decide?

Radical Changes in the Death Environment

Significant changes are taking place in our society's legal proscriptions against suicide, assisted suicide, and euthanasia. Mounting evidence suggests that a major shift in public opinion is also taking place away from the traditional Christian condemnation of suicide.

Changes in Public Opinion

The prestigious *New England Journal of Medicine* recently published two articles on physician and public opinion about legalizing life-terminating practices. Both articles report on responses to questionnaires about the legitimacy of assisted suicide. One recounts the responses of two Michigan populations, physicians and adult citizens. Respondents were asked to choose among three options: legalization of physician-assisted suicide, an explicit ban on the practice, or no law either permitting or prohibiting the practice. "Most Michigan physicians prefer either the legalization of physician-assisted suicide or no law at all; fewer than one-fifth prefer a complete ban on the practice. Given a choice between legalization and a ban, two-thirds of the Michigan public prefer legalization, and one-quarter prefer a ban."[8]

The second article focuses on physicians practicing in Oregon after the passage of the Oregon Death with Dignity Act, which legalized physician-assisted suicide. "Sixty percent of the respondents thought physician-assisted suicide should be legal in some cases, and nearly half might be willing to prescribe a legal dose of medication. Thirty-one percent of the respondents would be unwilling to do so on moral grounds."[9]

Changing Legal Response

Public disclosure about euthanasia moved directly into the political arena in November 1991, when Washington state voters were asked to accept a citizens' ballot proposal, Initiative 119, to make Washington the first jurisdiction in the Western world to legalize euthanasia.[10] The measure failed by a vote of 699,564 to 604,494. However, in November 1994, the state of Oregon did pass a Death with Dignity Act that allows legalized physician-assisted suicide.

The defeat of the Washington state legislation proved to be the beginning of a legal as well as a religious controversy that is still troublesome. Five years after the defeat of the legislation, an organization named Compassion in Dying approached the legitimization of assisted suicide through the courts, rather than through the ballot box. Their case was brought by three terminally ill patients, one a physician. In March of 1996, the state of Washington again made history when, on second appeal, the 9th Circuit Court found that the rights of terminally ill patients outweigh the state's legitimate interests in preventing suicide. This was the first time the right to die was found to be constitutional by a federal Appellate Court. The ruling affected a number of western states.

A few weeks later, the 2nd Circuit Court in New York upheld the right of persons to terminate their lives with physician assistance. Recently, several lawsuits have been filed, charging "wrongful life," meaning that persons have been kept alive against their will. In one suit, the patient had signed an advance directive, on her doctor's advice, when it became evident that she soon would be completely incapacitated. However, she and her mother were unable to stop treatment, and the woman was put on a ventilator, tube-fed, and maintained through a two-month coma. The family won a $16.5 million verdict in 1996.[11]

These decisions and others like them are chapters in a legal debate that probably will result in a U.S. Supreme

Court decision on the matter. However, a ruling by the highest court in the land is likely to be no more definitive than the *Roe vs. Wade* decision proved to be, as it relates to the continuing religious and political debate over abortion. Passionate religious discourse, as well as numerous legal maneuvers, give evidence to society's ambivalence about the wisdom of reshaping its moral code to respond to radical changes in the "death environment" that confronts contemporary America. A definitive set of values and patterns of social organization have yet to gain acceptance, though the old ones seem less than satisfactory.

Thirty years ago, the eminent ethicist Walter G. Muelder quoted Chief Justice Earl Warren in making his argument that law cannot exist without ethics: "In civilized life, law floats in a sea of ethics. Each is indispensable to civilization. Without law, we should be at the mercy of the least scrupulous; without ethics, law could not exist."[12] Current changes in legal interpretation suggest that our society is in the process of developing a new understanding of appropriate, responsible behavior on the part of those attending the death of persons whose lives can be prolonged almost indefinitely through high-tech medical intervention.

Religious Leaders Must Become Involved

Accounts of legal cases related to suicide and assisted suicide, as recorded in the secular press, might lead the reader to believe the conflict is a secular one between the state and health-care professions.

Only occasionally is there mention of the moral and spiritual questions involved. When religious commentary is considered newsworthy, it usually involves condemnation of changes in our legal code. For example, several newspapers carried an item about Bishop Fabian Bruskewitz of the Roman Catholic Diocese in Lincoln, Nebraska, who threatened to excommunicate persons associated with a number of organizations, including the Hemlock Society, which supports doctor-assisted suicide.[13]

A clergyperson with a different opinion made the news during the numerous lawsuits against Jack Kevorkian, M.D., who has been so public and vocal in his willingness to assist patients who want to end their lives. The foreman of the Michigan jury that acquitted this physician at a trial in the spring of 1996 was United Methodist Bishop Donald Ott. At the time of this trial, Dr. Kevorkian had admitted assisting in the deaths of 27 people.

Responses to Bishop Ott's role were mixed. Many religious persons expressed surprise that a Christian clergyperson would publicly espouse assisted suicide. As one Christian ethicist put it, "I'm sure the prosecution in the case wishes they had examined the potential jurors more closely!"[14] Other persons were distressed that the Bishop became involved in secular matters at all, believing that the separation of church and state means that no clergy should participate in such decision-making.

What should have interested the religious community about Bishop Ott was the value of his willingness to accept his civic responsibility to participate in community discourse and decision-making. It seems clear that he, and most persons who take their religious faith seriously, agree with Rabbi A. James Rubin that the changing technological and cultural context in which we live and die is forcing clergy and laity alike to reexamine their beliefs about suicide, assisted suicide, and euthanasia.

Suddenly the hospital room has become the locus for
moral and spiritual questions once discussed in abstraction within synagogues and churches. Ministers, rabbis,
priests and other religious authorities are going to have
to learn to function as effectively in this moral arena as
they do in their own houses of worship. . . . If clergy [and
we would add laity] are not prepared to confront the
moral and ethical dilemmas in our hospitals . . . critical
bioethical decisions about life and death will be made
solely by others. Religion would be cut out of the
process. And that would compound the tragedy.[15]

Tensions of Uncertainty

Some in the religious community interpret shifting
public opinion as an erosion of our traditional
Jewish/Christian religious leadership's role as monitors
of society's moral code. Others emphasize the crum-
bling of consensus within the religious community as a
sign of hope that religious leadership is beginning to
deal realistically and responsibly with a critical issue.
The ideological split among Christians divides the
churches along much the same lines as the abortion
debate. Some liberal Protestant denominations, for
example, appear increasingly to accept euthanasia. The
United Church of Christ and the Unitarian Universalist
Association have gone on record as affirming the right
of terminally ill persons to choose death over life, and
similar legislation may be introduced to the governing
bodies of other denominations in the near future. On
the other hand, most evangelical and fundamentalist
churches, along with the Roman Catholic Church, continue to maintain that active euthanasia is murder.

Any major shift in the moral attitude of a large por-
tion of the Christian community, as well as the larger
secular community, deserves the serious attention of all

religious leaders, theologians, and ethicists. However, developing new criteria concerning suicide is an awesome and difficult task. Religious leaders of diverse opinion can lead the way by debating publicly the mutability of moral law—that is, can traditional sanctions against suicide be lifted? If so, how and under what circumstances? Abstract, absolute statements about wrongful and rightful death are coherent when read from books or pronounced from pulpits. However, they become difficult to apply in real life-and-death situations when one stands at the bedside of a loved one. Likewise, they are difficult for nurses and physicians who work with patients and their families.

Several years of our collective experience in hospices, local churches, a school of medicine, and a school of theology convince us that simply rejecting the traditional absolute proscriptions may lessen tensions for some families and health-care providers, but it also creates new anxieties. When the religious rules are ambiguous, an added burden of uncertainty is evoked in caretakers, family members, and patients themselves. Some may experience feelings of guilt and depression. Other conscientious Christians searching for new guidelines run the risk of being criticized for having "abandoned their principles" as they adjust to contemporary cultural conditions, or of "idolizing" their belief in personal autonomy.

A Time for Cooperative Efforts to Discern God's Will

Against this backdrop of public concern, confusion, and fluctuating attitudes, we offer this book as our contribution to the thoughtful dialogue we believe must take place as our society responds to a technological medical environment in which human beings can be kept alive much longer than in previous times—in some cases, indefinitely. Society is reformulating its normative structure related to end-of-life issues. Dialogue about the reformulation must include theological and ethical considerations by a variety of discussants in order to develop a trustworthy normative structure. Legal experts, health-care providers, patients, and patient families, as well as ethicists and theologians must be involved.

The focus of our effort is to bring together writings by religious scholars, local church clergy, and pastoral counselors who work with the dying. These are offered to readers for study and debate. We pray that those who use this book will find information, analysis, and attitudes that will aid them in their own journey toward decisions about appropriate, responsible ways for persons of faith to die in our high-tech medical environment.

We are mindful of the roles that all communities of faith, including Jewish, Muslim, Hindu, Buddhist, as well as others, will play in the public discussion. Inter-religious and cross-cultural dialogue are welcomed. However, our focus is limited to the faith we know best.[16]

The ten authors whose works appear in this book reflect the reality of a conflicted Christian community which does not speak with one voice. If readers are to find answers to their questions about appropriate ways to die, it will be through engagement with a diverse assortment of responsible perspectives. We are proud to be able to offer works by outstanding persons. Our authors come from a variety of faith communities: Roman Catholic, United Methodist, Evangelical Free Church of America, and Presbyterian U.S.A. They are male and female, African American and European American, and they represent some of the best religious thinking available today.

Finally, we remind you that the editors and authors of

this book offer it in humility, for none of us has yet personally confronted death. Our answers are, at best, partial and incomplete. May your faith and ours sustain us all with God's grace as we continue our journey.

> Step lightly, we're walking home now.
> The clouds take every shape.
> We climb up the boulders; there is no plateau.
> We cross the stream and walk up the slope.
> See, the hawk is diving.
> The plain stretches out ahead,
> then the hills, the valleys, the meadows.
> Keep moving, people. How could I not be among you?[17]

NOTES

1. Lewis Thomas, "On Natural Death," in *The Medusa and the Snail: More Notes of a Biology Watcher* (New York: Bantam Books, 1986; Viking, 1979), p. 883.
2. Father Alexander M. Lukens died at the age of ninety-one, about a year after he sent me the Lewis Thomas quotation. A week before he died, he told me he was serene and ready.
3. William Fielding Ogburn, *Social Change* (New York: Viking, 1922, 1950). A succinct description of Ogburn's theory can be found in Melvin DeFluer, et al., *Sociology: Man in Society* (Glenview, Ill.: Scott Forseman, 1971), p. 193.
4. Ruth L. Fuller, M.D., is on the faculty of the Department of Psychiatry, University of Colorado Health Sciences Center. She serves as Director of the Pediatric Psychiatry liaison service at University Hospital, which includes consultation to the Sickle Cell Center, the Hemophilia Center, and the Neonatal Intensive Care Unit. She also has served as an advisor to the Hospice of Metro Denver and was a member of the Governor's Commission on Ethics and the Law.
5. Jeanette Modrick, "Physician Assistance in Dying: The Psychologist's Role and Women's Experience," unpublished paper. She quoted S. Miles and A. August, "Court, Gender and the 'Right to Die' " in *Law, Medicine, and Health Care*, 18, 1990, pp. 1-2.
6. Dietrich Bonhoeffer, *Ethics*, trans. Neville Horton Smith (New York: MacMillan Co., 1955), p. 163. The statement takes on a special meaning when one remembers the cultural milieu in which Bonhoeffer spoke. Recently I read Robert Jay Lifton's *Nazi Doctors* and visited the Holocaust Museum in Washington, D.C. While there, I thought about Bonhoeffer's defiance of evil and his concern for human life.
7. Reinhold Niebuhr, *The Nature and Destiny of Man, Vol. II* (New York: Charles Scribner's Sons, 1943), p. 293.

8. Jerald G. Bachman et al., "Attitudes of Michigan Physicians and the Public Toward Legalizing Physician-Assisted Suicide and Voluntary Euthanasia," *The New England Journal of Medicine*, Vol. 334, February 1, 1996, pp. 303-9.

9. Melinda A. Lee, et al., "Legalizing Assisted Suicide— Views of Physicians in Oregon," *The New England Journal of Medicine*, Vol. 334, February 1, 1996, pp. 210-15.

10. Public policy in the Netherlands tolerates physician-assisted suicide. However, there is no legislation that explicitly affirms the practice.

11. Tamar Lewin, "Wrongful Life Suits Filed," *The New York Times*, reprinted in *The Denver Post*, June 2, 1996. The article reports that besides the Young case, lawsuits have been filed recently in Arkansas and California.

12. Earl Warren, Address at the Jewish Theological Seminary of America, New York, November 1962, as quoted in Walter G. Muelder, *Moral Law in Christian Social Ethics* (Richmond: John Knox Press, 1966), p. 22.

13. Virginia Culver, "Threat of Ban Stirs Passion for Catholics," *The Denver Post*, March 28, 1996.

14. J. Philip Wogaman, "Assisted Suicide: the Moral Dilemma," *Wogaman Commentaries*, an on-line commentary produced by United Methodist News Service, Nashville, Tenn., New York, and Washington D.C., April 1, 1996.

15. A. James Rudin, "Clergy Aren't Prepared for Moral Dilemmas in the Hospital Room," *United Methodist Reporter*, April 19, 1996, p. 4.

16. Some portions of this chapter appeared earlier in *Christianity and Crisis:* Sally B. Geis, "The Church, the Bible and Suicide," Vol. 51, September 23, 1991, pp. 292-95; "The Meaning of Death: Time to Talk," Vol. 52, February 3, 1992, pp. 9-10.

17. Ted Rosenthal, "How Could I Not Be Among You?" in *Death: Current Perspectives*, ed. Edwin S. Shneidman (Palo Alto, Calif.: Mayfield Publishing Company, 1980).

Items for Reflection

1. What experiences have you, your family, or friends had with life-termination decisions? What questions and conflicts arose for you? What faith resources are you aware of? How helpful were they?
2. Discuss whether a Christian has a moral right to determine his or her own time and type of death, or whether this is a matter to be left in "the hands" of God.
3. The chapter suggests that each human life and death is the result of a complex variety of psychological, socioeconomic, spiritual, and cultural factors. For example, how might persons in poverty respond differently from affluent persons to the suggestion that each human being has the right to control her or his own quality of life?

CHAPTER TWO

Patient Refusal of Treatment

Cornish R. Rogers &
Nigel M. de S. Cameron

ROBERT OLMSTEAD
"I've been thinking about my father a lot lately. Six weeks ago he fell and fractured a vertebra in his spine. Cancer had weakened it. Now there is evidence of cancer throughout his body. The oncologist described what comes next—biopsies, chemotherapy, radiation treatment, physical therapy. On Thursday night, my father told them, 'No!' No more tests. No more treatments.

"As my father has grown older and more hard of hearing, he has tended to think things through to himself and then announce what he thinks, sometimes entirely out of context with what others are talking about. The last time I visited him, he obviously had been thinking about things.

"Among other things, he said, 'I feel much closer to God now. Jesus seems especially close. I know that no matter what happens, Jesus is accompanying me.' It was out of character for my father to speak that intimately, but he did."*

---

* Sermon by Robert Olmstead, First United Methodist Church, Palo Alto, California, quoted by Donald J. Shelby, "The Only Way to Go," May 28, 1995.

Patient Refusal of Treatment

Cornish R. Rogers

The musical *Kiss of the Spiderwoman* features two political prisoners in a Brazilian jail cell during the height of an oppressive regime. One man is tortured in an attempt to force him to reveal the time and place of a suspected act of sedition. The other prisoner is secretly asked by the authorities to befriend the first man, in order to persuade him to provide the needed information. Torture abounds in the prison, with blood-curdling screams and the dragging of mutilated bodies past their cells.

But with intermittent regularity, a phantom Spiderwoman dances and flits over a giant web, constructed partly of the steel bars of the cells. She sings invitingly to the prisoners to come to her when they can no longer stand the torture. She, of course, is the figure of death, and according to the theater notes, "embodies the essential feminine persona that inhabits the life of both men."[1]

The men stubbornly resist the seductive gestures of the Spiderwoman until the prisoner who was asked to cooperate with the authorities refuses to give up the information asked for, chooses death, and embraces the Spiderwoman.

Death: Last Outpost of Freedom

While that story does not fully parallel the case study, it does illustrate the absolute necessity for us to be able to choose death when we deem it preferable to a meaningless or compromised life. Death is the last outpost of freedom.

The decision on the part of a patient to refuse treatment of an ostensible terminal illness depends largely upon the patient's fitness to think clearly and to prepare in advance for that "undiscovered country from whose bourne no traveler has returned."[2]

It was interesting to note that Robert Olmstead recalled how his father had thought through his mortality for some time before making his decision to refuse treatment for the cancer that progressively invaded his body. Only someone who knew him over a period of time could have understood and respected the decision he made, however much they might have disagreed.

That is the crux of the issue; while I believe the patient does have the freedom to refuse treatment in such a case, it is the responsibility of those who love the patient to help the patient understand the implications of his or her decision. Moreover, the patient's friends and relatives bear some responsibility for providing the opportunity for the patient's spiritual development.

By spiritual development, I mean the exploration of one's relationship to the intangible realities of life in God, and their appropriation for one's life here and now. The patient's decision should be grounded in a field of experience that locates the patient in the context of his or her place in God's kingdom. That cannot be accomplished, however, without a community of persons who surround the patient with love and a sense of belonging. That is why the church is such an important institution in our lives, although other communities of concern also can provide that function in one's life.

Hamlet's soliloquy, quoted in part above, exposes our natural fear of dying by making us "bear those ills we have, than fly to others we know not of."[3] That fear, and our natural instinct for life combine to present a formidable defense against any arbitrary decision to end one's life. So when one does make the decision to be allowed to die, and evinces a modicum of sanity, he or she must be taken seriously.

Fearing Loss of Control and Dignity

In the past, intractable pain was a major reason for
terminally ill patients wanting to die, but it was not the
fear of pain that motivated Robert Olmstead's father to
refuse treatment. In fact, today pain is largely controllable. It appears instead that he feared more the loss of
control and dignity, and the financial dependence often
associated with the end stage of fatal illness.

A recent *Los Angeles Times* editorial quoted a Washington State study of doctor-assisted suicide and
euthanasia which concluded: "Notably, neither severe
pain nor dyspnea (shortness of breath) was a common
patient concern, suggesting that intolerable physical
symptoms are not the reason most patients request
physician-assisted suicide or euthanasia." A court ruling
opined: "A competent terminally ill adult, having lived
nearly the full measure of his life, has a strong liberty
interest in choosing a dignified and humane death,
rather than being reduced at the end of his existence to a
childlike state of helplessness, diapered, sedated, incompetent." [4]

The Right of Deciding When to Die

There is a growing recognition in church circles of the
legitimacy of the rights of patients to decide when to
die. The Episcopal Diocese of Newark has recently
adopted a resolution calling suicide "a moral choice" for
the terminally ill. Donald Ott, a United Methodist bishop who served as foreman of the jury in Pontiac, Michigan, that acquitted Dr. Jack Kevorkian of illegally aiding
suicides, once wrote that "choosing the time of one's
death in a terminal condition can be an expression of
faithful living." [5]

But this growing societal shift points to a critical failure of the church in preparing the faithful for death. If we are to support terminal patients' freedom to decide when to die, whether by refusal of treatment or by other means, we have the moral responsibility to prepare them for their eventual death. Dr. C. Everett Koop, the former U.S. Surgeon General, said: "One of the great problems in our mobile society has to do with the decisions at the end of life." [6] He suggested that we think about how we want to die, and have a frank talk about it with our families.

Henri Nouwen, the celebrated Dutch mystic, calls us to "befriend" our death. In *Our Greatest Gift*, a meditation on dying and caring, he writes:

> Is death something so terrible and absurd that we are better off not thinking or talking about it? Is death such an undesirable part of our existence that we are better off acting as if it were not real? Is death such an absolute end of all our thoughts and actions that we simply cannot face it? Or is it possible to befriend our dying gradually and live open to it, trusting that we have nothing to fear? Is it possible to prepare for our death with the same attentiveness that our parents had in preparing for our birth? Can we wait for our death as for a friend who wants to welcome us home? [7]

Preparing for one's death is not a morbid activity, but a caring one. It can be a fully satisfactory experience of taking care of one's responsibility to others, of making sure that issues that will affect others after your passing are resolved, or making plans for the continuation of care to those dependent on you. But the greatest satisfaction comes in reconciling with those from whom you have been estranged or in conflict.

Terminal patients who have had the opportunity to "befriend" their dying can be trusted to decide when to refuse treatment to extend their lives, for instead of being an enemy, death becomes a friend.

Jesus' Decision to Die

In a very real sense, Jesus was faced with the decision of whether to preserve his life or submit to the Roman authorities and be executed. In that memorable Garden of Gethsemane incident recorded in the Gospels, Jesus prays for God's will as to whether he should live or die, confessing frankly his desire to continue living. However, sensing God's will in the context of his mission and ministry, Jesus chose to die.

Although the context was not that of a terminal illness or chronic pain, Jesus exercised his freedom to make that decision, based upon what he considered the right thing to do, as he understood God's will. It is that same God-given freedom that a terminal patient can exercise to refuse treatment to prolong his or her life. Without that freedom, a person cannot make a moral choice. To be sure, it is altogether possible that the wrong choice is made, but it is a moral choice, nevertheless.

Does it not seem unfair for God to thrust us, without our permission, into a life of mortality, and forbid us to escape from it, if it becomes unbearable or without meaningful purpose? Can not we, like Jesus, decide when to let go when our death can serve a greater good than our living? That is undoubtedly what Martin Luther King, Jr., meant when he reminded us that unless we are willing to die for something, we are not fit to live. There is no freedom in life unless we can decide when to end it, even for a less than noble purpose. Ending our life is an exercise of moral freedom.

Responsible Use of the Right to Die

With every freedom, however, is the responsibility of its rightful use. Choosing to refuse treatment in a terminal illness involves more persons than the one who is ill. Loved ones, both relatives and friends, have a vital stake in such a decision. As mentioned at the outset, the Olmstead family and friends should help him think through such a decision.

First of all, they should let him know how much they love him and want him with them, but that they will honor his decision because they love him.

Second, they ought to have him talk about why he has decided to refuse treatment. Is it because of too much pain, or depression, or hopelessness about ever recovering adequately, or is he just tired of living?

Third, they ought to ask him to postpone his decision until he has prayed about it to seek God's will, and until he has had a good night's rest, if that is possible.

Fourth, they should ask him if he has his "house" in order and is ready to die in peace.

Finally, they should once again express their love for him and wish him Godspeed!

NOTES

1. Manuel Puig, *Kiss of the Spiderwoman,* trans. Thomas Colchie (New York: Knopf, 1979), theatre notes.
2. Shakespeare, *Hamlet* (New York: Groset Dunlap, Cameo Classics, 1909), Act III, Scene i, line 79-80.
3. Shakespeare, *Hamlet* (Act) III. (Scene) i.
4. *Los Angeles Times,* April 8, 1996.
5. *United Methodist Review,* April 5, 1996, p. 1.
6. *Parade Magazine,* April 7, 1996, p. 3.
7. Henri J. M. Nouwen, *Our Greatest Gift* (HarperSanFrancisco, 1994), pp. xii-xiii.

Patient Refusal of Treatment

Nigel M. de S. Cameron

This brief case highlights in a moving and realistic fashion the practical dimension which any discussion of end-of-life issues must face: of all ethical dilemmas, our subjects in this volume are most likely to come laden with anguish and distress unique in the experience of those involved. Ethics must here be incarnated in the practical and sometimes harrowing facts of experience. When Robert Olmstead says, "I've been thinking about my father a lot lately," all of us (whether our fathers are dead or alive) know something of what he means. In present experience, retrospect, or prospect, we are one with him in the ambivalences of aging, death, and filial piety. As we read the Olmstead case, we think of the decisions that ultimately await our fathers, mothers, children, and ourselves.

The Need to Know More

At the same time, we want to know more about the writer, about his father, whose faith shines through his declaration of confidence in Jesus Christ, and whose desire to be with him—"far better," said Paul—is already invading his spirit as cancer invades his body. And *we wish*—especially as we write and read these chapters—that we knew more about the case. In fact, these short paragraphs, moving and reflective as they are, also seem very short on the kind of information which we assume the Olmsteads had at their ready disposal, and which, if we are to offer a review of the rights and wrongs of their situation, would be helpful to us.

We know that Olmstead senior is old (but 60? 80?), growing deaf, affected perhaps by early dementia (his

behavior is certainly changing), but also more conscious of the great questions of life and death. We know
he has fallen, and that a cancer diagnosis has followed—"throughout his body," we read. The oncologist
is ready to invoke the armamentarium of the trade:
biopsies, chemotherapy, radiation, with physical therapy to follow. The unanswered question—really rather
central to our discussion—is, what is the prognosis?
Since biopsies are still in view, is there one yet? That
is, is the oncologist who already has diagnosed "cancer
throughout his body" yet in a position to know
whether an aggressive treatment regime is indicated? If
so—that is, if he or she has made that judgment
already—what are the implied conclusions as to the
outcomes on which these various courses of treatment
are being recommended?

Determining Whether Treatment Is Appropriate

That is what lies at the heart of this discussion: the
question of whether treatment is appropriate or
whether (conversely) it is futile; whether, in traditional
medical parlance, it is "indicated" when set on a proper
scale of burdens and benefits. At the one extreme, the
patient is dying and soon will be dead; these invasive
exercises will have no significant effect on that outcome or its timing; and supposedly therapeutic treatments would be an outrage and a fraud, since they
would be entirely futile (they would not bring about
their intended ends) and, what is more and quite dis-
tinct, in some respects, of great discomfort to a dying
man. At the other extreme, of course, we have a treatment which, in the general course of things, will very
likely lead to full recovery and a restoration of the state
of health in which the patient was found when first
diagnosed.

The problem in so many situations, of course, is that we are somewhere in the middle. Indeed, it may not be at all clear just where a given case is located, or different specialists may take different views, or there may be an underlying condition (such as Alzheimer's or perhaps the effects of stroke) which causes uncertainty as to the nature and worthwhileness of the "health" to which the patient is being "restored." All these factors are relevant, and often present.

Nonetheless, if we cannot seek at the level of principle for some clarity in our understanding of the interface of ethical and clinical judgments, we are lost; that is to say, we consign our decisions in this most poignant life experience to the immediacy of the moment and the pressures of the individuals, the insurers, and the hospital, and recent news-magazine articles which emerge at a time of personal trial. And at the level of principle, there are some certainties:

1. Futile treatment, hard though it may be to define in some cases (though easy in others), should not be attempted; if it has been, and is then judged to be futile, it should be withdrawn.
2. Treatment that is judged beneficial, on an accounting of benefits and burdens (again, sometimes hard, sometimes easy) is treatment that should be given.
3. The judgment of the individual patient concerned, and his or her relatives or other companions or proxy, has a key though problematic place in the assessment. Though we do not know much about Olmstead senior, our brief account does suggest that this is the key question here: Whatever the prognosis and its grounding, he wants to trump it with his own decision. And his decision is, "No!"

Issues of Life and Death

Let us first review the background to the case. What are the principal issues of life and death that lie behind all such personal and medical dilemmas?

Recent appeals decisions, which presumably will meet final resolution in the Supreme Court, threaten to create in the United States the first major euthanasia jurisdiction in the modern world, in which refusal-of-treatment decisions of this kind would be overwhelmed in an option for "treatment" whose candid purpose is to kill (to be fair, Australia's Northern Territory seems technically to be the first; in the Netherlands, public policy favors euthanasia and has for two decades, though it remains technically illegal). Jack Kevorkian has become a sinister household name through his exercise of "physician-assisted suicide," a soft version of euthanasia. A fresh (and cost-saving) option could soon be added in the clinical management of the sick. As our tradition of consensus medicine continues to fracture, initiatives like those are being driven like wedges into the common ground that remains. Many who favor them little foresee the consequences of the earthquake they may soon trigger, as the stress grows on faultlines which have not shifted since Hippocrates laid down the ethical foundations of Western medicine.

Let us look at some definitions before we go further. Recent debate has been deliberately focused on "physician-assisted suicide," offered as the very mildest form of euthanasia, since it labels it as suicide rather than homicide. Interestingly, it is just this form that is explicitly ruled out in the Hippocratic Oath, the basis of 2,000 years of Western medicine: "I will not give poison to anyone though asked to do so, nor will I suggest such a plan." And remember: That bold statement was made at a time when drug therapies were in their infancy, and no one had heard of hospice.

Yet is "physician-assisted suicide" really suicide? The purpose of describing an act as suicide is to make plain that the culprit and the victim are one and the same. Yet if the physician employs his professional skills with the intent of bringing about the patient's death, even at his request and irrespective of who places the tablet (provided by the physician) in his mouth, we see, at least, the telltale signs of homicide as well as suicide, do we not? Given the physician's duty of care, and (by definition) the weakened state of the sick patient, if physician-assisted is really suicide, it is certainly homicide as well. They don't somehow cancel each other out, or produce a third kind of act, neither one thing nor the other. They are added to each other, overlaid as (in traditional medicine as well as in Christian ethics) very serious moral evils.

"Euthanasia" is not easy to define. The word, of course, simply means "good death," and was first used to speak of a natural death free of distress. It was then hijacked as a term for death that results from someone's decision to end a life, in the context of medical care. Because of the built-in ambiguity (good death/death from choice) we must be careful to distinguish it from aspects of medicine we have always considered good; stopping treatment when it becomes counter-productive (no longer "beneficial" to the patient), and (often in the same situation) using pain-relieving drugs, even though they may shorten life as a side effect. Neither of these is euthanasia, since in neither case is there an act or an omission intended to bring about death. Euthanasia requires such an intention (in the case of voluntary euthanasia and physician-assisted suicide, insofar as they may be distinguished, two people's intention), that the patient's death should be contrived, as an object in his clinical management.

We speak of euthanasia as "active" and as "passive"

—by lethal injection, for example (active), or by failing to give life-saving treatment with a view to ending life (passive). Some people—especially proeuthanasia advocates—equate not treating or withdrawing treatment when treatment is not beneficial with passive euthanasia, but that is needlessly confusing. There is a gray area between the two, but in principle the intention of the attending physician is either simply to recognize that treatment is no longer effective in healing/sustaining life, or to cause death. If the latter is no part of the physician's intention, the act is not one of euthanasia.

Much is made of the distinction between "voluntary" and "involuntary" euthanasia, and euthanasia advocates are eager to distinguish the two—and to deny that they favor the latter, though the more closely it is examined, the thinner the distinction proves to be. That focuses our attention on the key practical problem of voluntary euthanasia in the guise of physician-assisted suicide: the problem of the volunteer. If we leave aside the major ethical questions and assume (a) that suicide is okay; and (b) that the physician's involvement in homicide is okay, then we see that everything depends on (c), the underlying justification of the process in the autonomy of the patient and his right to determine when and how he dies.

We do not need to examine the typical situation very long to realize that we face serious difficulties here. As already pointed out, the patient, in most euthanasia scenarios, is in chronic or terminal illness. That has deep-seated implications for his exercise of value-free choice in something as vastly important as his own death. When patients ask to be helped to die, as sometimes they do, the good physician has always addressed the question of possible depression, problems of relationships and worries among family and friends, whether the treatment is really the best available (especially in pain control), and so on. The option of death on request short-circuits that whole process, and also avoids the issue of whether the patient properly understands the prognosis, how he will feel in the later stages of the disease, how family and friends will react—maybe for many years—to a suicide decision, and of course, the moral issues involved.

But let us assume that the patient is a professor of medicine who has lately moved into bioethics, and therefore understands the questions; and let us assume that her prognosis is clear. What then? Well, how many sick and elderly people feel that their children would really prefer them dead? Or, whatever they would prefer, that with them dead, their children would be better off emotionally and financially? And what about the children who do feel that way, and pressure the patient into such a choice? And what about the doctor—the doctor whose very acceptance of playing a part in the suicide/euthanasia process gives it legitimacy to his patient, suggesting that it may be an appropriate response to financial and other concerns?

There are other practical problems, many of which have become evident in the one country where euthanasia is being widely practiced (though, as we have noted, it is technically illegal). In Holland, the theory is that patients must first ask for death before the doctor acts. In fact, doctors confidentially admit to many cases of active killing of patients who have never made a request (around one in four cases), and seniors in care facilities are becoming frightened of contact with doctors.

And what of the impact of all this on the health-care professionals themselves? Most physicians in Holland now have been involved in taking patients' lives, but some have been outspoken in their resistance. Legalization would require every physician to be involved, at least in referral. A new duty is created for the physician.

If it is my right to ask for death as a health-care option, it becomes my physician's duty to provide it; and, of course, the duty of nurses and others to assist.

Why Christians Oppose Killing

These anguished practical reflections bring us directly to the central ethical issue. These are solid theological reasons why Christians have been so opposed to killing. Life is sacred because humankind is made in the image of God. Christians have always held that the killing of ourselves is wrong, for the same reason that the killing of others is wrong: The image sets human life apart as that of persons who are constituted by the likeness to their Maker (Genesis 9:6). Life may not be taken, by others or ourselves, except in the strictly defined context of war and capital punishment. The general rule is clear: "The LORD gave, the LORD takes away" (Job 1:12). Of course, Job offers us much more than a prooftext, for he is presented to us as a human being defined by suffering; and yet we see a man of faith, for whom the combination of bereavement, sickness, and taunting of his friends does not lead him (as his wife suggests) to "curse God and die."

Which brings us back to Mr. Olmstead, for the plain legal distinction between suicide and simple refusal of treatment is not so straightforward in morals, where the suicidal intent of a refusal decision may be discernible. That must be distinguished from a refusal decision based on the futility and inappropriateness of the treatment, and also (and more problematically) from one placed in the gray area where the outcomes are so unclear, or the likelihood of treatment so uncertain, as to free the patient or his or her advocate from any sense of obligation to be treated, yet without implying clear "futility." If the treatment refusal is unambiguously suicidal (when treatment is strongly indicated with a good prognosis), the physician and other attendants are placed in a specifically difficult position. The Christian commitment to the sanctity of life extends to our own life, as much as anyone else's. It does not entail inappropriate treatment, but it does suggest the need for courage and a determination to leave it to the God who gives life to decide to take it away.

STUDY GUIDE

What justification, if any, exists, for a person to refuse medical treatment and thus, in essence, terminate his or her own life?

Cornish R. Rogers argues that choosing to end one's own life, under certain circumstances, can represent "an exercise of moral freedom." Citing Jesus' decision to choose death over submitting to Roman authorities, Rogers says it is an "absolute necessity" for Christians to choose death when the alternative is "a meaningless or compromised life."

Nigel M. de S. Cameron insists that the "Christian commitment to the sanctity of life extends to our own life as much as anyone else's." Inappropriate, futile treatment is not required. However, we are called to courageously let our "God who gives life to decide to take it away." He uses the "wedge" or "slippery slope" argument that endorsing patient refusal of possibly beneficial treatment will lead inevitably to other acts that are morally objectionable, such as physician-assisted suicide (what he calls physician-assisted homicide).

Items for Reflection

1. Discuss whether any of the following conditions prompt you to favor the hastening of your own death or that of a loved one:
   - loss of control over functions such as feeding, bathing, and dressing?
   - loss of bladder and bowel control?
   - unremitting, severe pain that is uncontrollable?

2. Rogers suggests that terminally ill Christians should involve family and/or friends in the decision to refuse treatment. Do you think this is a good idea, or is such a decision a private matter to be decided by the patient alone, without "interference" from others?

3. In what ways does Jesus' choice of suffering death on a cross seem similar to or different from a person refusing medical treatment, and thus choosing death from disease?

4. What responsibility does a Christian have to investigate fully whether treatment is appropriate, before making a decision to refuse or terminate medical procedures?

5. Will the practice of endorsing a patient's refusal of treatment lead to the killing of persons who have not asked to die? What evidence supports this "slippery slope" argument?

CHAPTER THREE

Patient Decision for Withdrawal of Treatment

Bruce Hilton &
Lisa Sowle Cahill

Alfred was a Native American, born and raised on a tribal reservation. He served as a corporal in a combat unit during the Vietnam conflict. On his return, he moved to a large city, found work in a fast-food restaurant, and became an active member of a church in the neighborhood where he lived. About a year later, his friends began to notice that he was frequently ill with a fever and bad cough. Eventually, it became clear that he was quite ill. His church friends urged him to seek medical treatment, but Alfred did not trust Western medicine and did not want to seek help from doctors trained in that tradition.

Gradually he grew weaker, and one day he neither called nor appeared for work, so a co-worker went to his apartment, found Alfred unconscious on the floor, and called 911. The paramedics came, resuscitated him, and took him to the city hospital, where he was placed on a respirator. When he regained consciousness, he seemed agitated and tried to pull the tubes from his body. Medical personnel felt an obligation to do a complete workup on his case in order to reach a definitive diagnosis and determine the best treatment plan. These tests showed that he had widespread lymphoma that might possibly be treatable.

His friends knew that Alfred had talked recently

about having dreams of death. Though he had not left a note, many believed that he had tried to end his life with an overdose of drugs. They also were sure that he did not want to be treated in the white man's hospital to which he had been taken. However, the hospital refused to withdraw treatment.

But finally Alfred was able to free his hands and pull out all the tubes. Treatment was not resumed after this incident, and Alfred died a few days later. Many of his friends wondered whether he would have been better off if nobody had called 911 when he was found unconscious. Maybe then he would have died the way he wanted to die.*

---

* Composite case from the files of Ruth L. Fuller, M.D., an African American psychiatrist whose research interests include death in cross-cultural settings.

Patient Decision for Withdrawal of Treatment

Bruce Hilton

I think about sitting in a meeting of a hospital ethics committee, trying to see into the clouded mind of Annie J.

At seventy-eight, Annie J., once an active, outgoing woman, has been bedridden for six years. In that time she has come to the hospital at least once a year for pneumonia or infections, staying a month or more. Each time, her mind has been more clouded with Alzheimer's disease, her body more shaken with the tremors of Parkinson's disease. She has cancer of the uterus that has spread to other parts of her body, but seems to have slowed.

Her husband, Carl, has been a loving and attentive caregiver. She doesn't recognize him or what he's doing when he feeds her, a spoonful at a time, three meals a day. For the past year, despite Carl's care, she has been a patient in the skilled nursing facility (SNF or "sniff," in staff jargon) of a big-city hospital. That's because some of the food Carl gives her keeps getting in her windpipe, making her gag and choke. When enough of it gets into her lungs, she has another difficult bout of pneumonia. Meanwhile, she's barely getting enough to eat.

Annie has had the best of care. Radiation treatment slowed the cancer. Thin plastic hoses into veins in her arm and thigh carry three kinds of antibiotic, water, a painkiller, an antacid, and an antinausea drug. Another pair of tubes bring oxygen to her nostrils. She is no more aware of these miracles of high-tech medicine than of the diaper and catheter that have helped to keep her clean since she lost control of her bodily functions.

The Key Question

The ethics committee meets with some of Annie's doctors and nurses because those who give her care feel that Carl's love is holding her prisoner. On the one hand, he has asked the doctors for a "do-not-resuscitate" order, in case of cardiac arrest, and has refused tube feeding for her—a measure that would ease the choking and the pneumonia. On the other hand, he insists on continuing the oxygen, antibiotics, and IV fluids, and wants her transferred to an acute-care ward when crises hit. Foregoing any of these would make death likely.

At the ethics committee meeting, just as in Alfred's hospital room, plenty of people are ready to "let Mrs. J go." Some of these are nurses who have known her for years and have shown real concern for her comfort; some are doctors who feel it is cruel to "keep her going" in this mindless, undignified state. But the regular members of the committee keep pulling the discussion back to the key question—whether to withhold or withdraw life-extending medical treatment: *What does the patient want?*

It has taken decades to get to that question. As recently as the late 1960s, the idea of *not* doing everything humanly possible for a patient was not even discussed in medical journals. Virginia Hilton recalls a surgeon in 1972 who tried to have her fired as a supervising nurse for suggesting that it might be more humane to stop fighting for the life of a patient, a patient whose physical suffering was exacerbated by such severe erosion of his face that he wouldn't let his family see him.

If a decision occasionally was made to pull back on the treatment of a dying patient, it was done in private, by one person—the doctor. Most doctors viewed the death of a patient as professional failure. Few medical

schools taught the idea that the death rate, in this country or any other, is ultimately 100 percent.

What caused the change? History is complicated, but
two phenomena stand out: the human independence
movements of the 1960s and the rapid growth of technology in medicine.

The Movements

It's hard now to realize the power of the nonviolent
revolutions of the 1960s. Much history has been rewrit-
ten to make it seem as though the inmates took over
the asylum, that brainless youth challenged authority
just for the excitement of it.

In the long term, history will show that the bubbling
pot produced a pretty good stew. A thousand clergy
went to Mississippi in 1964 to help win the vote for
African Americans; they came back so sensitized to the
abuse of power everywhere that a third of them alienat-
ed their congregations and lost their pulpits within two
years. One goal of the women's movement was control
in matters of health; the plain and frank book, *Our Bodies, Our Selves*, gave them the necessary knowledge.
The participants in a series of minicampaigns varied
widely: the Free Speech movement, the more discrimi-
nating and insistent consumer, and the peaceful army
that ended the Vietnam conflict are examples. The
bumper sticker, "Question Authority," didn't cover all
that went on, but it came close.

The Technology

Meanwhile, the doctors' tools were getting more
sophisticated. They learned parenteral feeding—the ability to fine-tune nutrients that could be fed into a patient's
veins for months, even years. The ventilator (respirator)

could keep people breathing in a crisis—or a chronic failure lasting years. Radiation and chemotherapy helped fight cancer. Transplants seemed truly miraculous.

But the technology had unexpected side effects—ethical questions that doctors were ill-prepared to answer. When Robert F. Kennedy was shot in a Los Angeles hotel, ambiguous bulletins were issued from the hospital. The fact is that the candidate was dead, but the ventilator blurred the usual signs that death had occurred: cessation of breathing and heartbeat. *The doctors didn't know whether it was moral to withdraw the respirator.* Events like this led to new legal definitions of the time when death had occurred (total cessation of any brain activity).

In the late 1960s, medicine began to wrestle with the new syndromes: with technology's unexpected side effects, patients were no longer willing to be kept ignorant or powerless. In the early 1970s, some pioneering doctors and a few outsiders were raising questions about authority in medicine. A Harvard professor, Dr. Henry Beecher, documented dozens of cases of medical research in which patients' lives were endangered without their consent—"for the greater good." I was part of an investigative group that interviewed a Texas doctor who ran a family planning clinic, and in the name of research, gave placebos—sugar pills—to sixty Mexican American women who had come to him for birth control. The physician who invented kidney dialysis found that there would not be nearly enough machines to help everyone who needed dialysis; rather than make the decision himself, he set up a committee, *made up mostly of nondoctors,* to select the lucky ones who would live.

Three Important Ideas

A national commission for the protection of human subjects in medicine and research was created. Their sessions gave authority to three ideas that are important—not only to Alfred, not only to Annie J., but to you and me. They are *patient autonomy, informed consent,* and *weighing the burdens and the benefits of a proposed treatment.* Those concepts are at the heart of ethical decision making in most hospitals today. *What does the patient want?*

The United States is unique in its emphasis on autonomy, even at the expense of the common good (it has made us the only industrial nation without universal health care, for example). But the strength of the autonomy approach ("What does the patient want?") is that it is a defense against the abuse of power by those around the patient.

Who can judge the patient's quality of life? Not the doctor. Not the spouse. Not the son who hasn't called or written for years, but turns up when Dad is dying, demanding a full-court press. *Only the patient knows.* Only patients know their own values and priorities well enough to say, "I'll fight on," or "It's no longer worth going on; let me die naturally."

Steps in Decision Making

The courts have made it clear that the patient must be competent, has a right to be fully informed, and doesn't lose the right to refuse treatment when he or she becomes incompetent. The decision-making ladder that has developed over twenty-five years goes like this:

1. What does the patient say he or she wants?
2. If unconscious, what has he or she said or written about this in the past?
3. If unconscious and without a written or spoken directive, what is he or she likely to have decided, in the best judgment of those who would know?

4. If none of the above is available, then other agents—
caregivers, the hospital ethics committee, a clinical
ethicist—may decide. They will decide on a basis
entirely different from the three above: "What is in
the best interest of the patient?" This is where burdens (like pain and suffering) are weighed against
benefits (such as the chances of full recovery).

In Annie's case, the question is easy to answer. Back
when she was able, she told her husband many times
that she didn't want to be dependent on technology to
artificially extend her dying.

After the discussion, the ethics committee and staff
feel they know what is morally right: Obey her clearly
stated wish not to be in this position. Withdraw the
antibiotics, IV liquids, and other high-tech death-exten-
ders. But they also know that Carl J.'s whole life is
bound up in caring for his wife. He is the real patient.
The question the committee must now ponder is this:
How can we deal with Carl in a way that respects his
feelings and humanity while honoring Annie's wishes?

Discovering What Alfred Wanted

In Alfred's case, like so many in hospitals today, the
issues are even more complicated. In the first place,
many of those involved were asking the wrong questions. For example, the doctors wanted a definitive diagnosis "to determine the best treatment plan." That was
only part of the information needed. The tests would tell
them what they might be able to do for Alfred. But the
tests would not tell them what they *ought* to do. Ethics
dilemmas—the "should" and "ought" questions—are
not solved by science. The doctors needed to add the
phrase, " . . . if, in fact, Alfred *wants* to be treated."
Some, but not all, of Alfred's co-workers and friends

made the same kind of mistake—well-meaning, even loving, but a mistake just the same. They became caught up in discussions of what they thought was best for him.

The second cause of confusion was the lack of a clear, strong answer to the right question: *What does the patient want?*

There were some strong clues. When Alfred awoke in the hospital, he tried to pull out the respirator tube in his throat and the intravenous tubes in his arms. Friends said he had told them of dreaming about death. Some thought he once had tried suicide by an overdose. In some states, this might be enough to indicate a desire to die. In others, like Missouri and New York, there must be "clear and convincing evidence" before doctors are required to obey an unconscious patient's request to withdraw treatment. Alfred hadn't filled out an advance directive; he hadn't designated an agent to speak for him. Indeed, the case description leaves the strong impression that Alfred—like most Americans—had never had a discussion with friends or relatives who could confidently say, "*This* is what Alfred would have wanted."

There's a third complication: the question of whether Alfred was rejecting any and all treatment of his condition, or just Western medicine's approach to it.

We may have the best medical technology in the world, but we are coming to see that it is not the only way. And sometimes our insistence on our way can violate Hippocrates' warning to doctors: "First, do no harm." Not far from where I live, a seventeen-year-old girl, an immigrant from Southeast Asia, was diagnosed with cancer. After an uncomfortable course of chemotherapy, she refused a second course, saying she would rather be treated by the shaman of her Hmong community. When she persisted, the sheriff sent more than a dozen deputies to take her from her home and

transport her to the hospital, where she had the intravenous treatment under armed guard.

On the day a third set of treatments was scheduled,
she disappeared. People are still asking whether it
wouldn't have been better—healthier, even—to respect
her autonomy as a near-adult, and her religious beliefs
in how the body heals.

It's sad that none of Alfred's friends seemed to be in a
position to help him find native healers. It's sad that the
hospital couldn't find a way to bring in a healer or
shaman acceptable to Alfred, to work alongside the
Western doctors. You might be surprised to know how
often modern doctors, aware that most healing is still a
mystery, are opening the door to such cooperation. If
Alfred was not clear about dying, he certainly was clear
about his discomfort with high-tech medicine. The outcome might have been different, had enough people
heard his clear answer to the question: *What does the
patient want?*

Hindsight is usually 20/20; certainly no finger of
blame is here pointed at the people who tried to help
Alfred. But oh, they did miss the opportunities to
respect his wishes. For example:

- When he began to be seriously ill, friends might have
  encouraged and helped in a search for native healing,
  or a doctor willing to work with a traditional healer.
- Was the co-worker who found Alfred unconscious one
  of those who were sure he wanted to die? If so, he or
  she might have honored that wish by refusing to call
  911.
- When Alfred tried to pull out his tubes, the hospital
  bound his arms—"for his own protection," one
  assumes. I've seen it many times; all too often the
  struggle is a strong message: "Enough of this! Let me
  go!" All too often, it is a message ignored.
- When friends were sure Alfred did not want to be

treated in that hospital, but didn't press the idea of other forms of healing, they missed another chance.

- When the hospital refused to withdraw treatment, friends and co-workers might have called for a meeting of the hospital ethics committee. Anybody can make this call, and most hospitals have well-trained committees eager to help. Their members usually include medical professionals, community representatives, and specialists in bioethics. They are often a patient's best defense against institutional inertia, habit, professional egotism, and the pervasive, unreasoning fear of lawsuit.

It is to the credit of those involved that when Alfred pulled out the tubes a second time, everybody finally "heard" him. In his suffering, he refused to let them ignore any longer the key question in the withdrawal of medical treatment:

What does the patient want?

Patient Decision for Withdrawal of Treatment

Lisa Sowle Cahill

Alfred's case poignantly explains the momentum behind the "assisted-suicide" movement in our nation today. Caught with no practical alternative other than entrusting his fate to intensive, hi-tech, institutional medicine, he chooses death. Maybe he intentionally overdosed on drugs; he definitely pulled out treatment tubes, over the resistance of would-be caregivers. The case's last line is ironic: If Alfred had been left to die alone in his apartment, "maybe then he would have died the way he wanted to die." In fact, Alfred's choice to die (whether by an overdose or by refusing treatment) was a desperate act, an act of avoidance of a worse destiny, as well as resistance to conditions that made living a terrifying prospect. There is little doubt that his so-called "choice" was an act of hopelessness, not the fulfillment of personal aspirations or the culmination of a meaningful life plan.

Divergent Worldviews and Relationships

This man's Native American identity is a theme that resonates throughout the case. Raised within his tribe, he is plucked from his roots by Vietnam, and now finds himself employed in that epitome of anonymity, that contradiction to meal as ritual of family, companionship, and hospitality: a fast-food restaurant in a large city. No passive victim of his circumstances, however, Alfred seeks out community in a neighborhood church, where he makes friends who remain concerned with his welfare.

Alfred's encounter with illness and eventual death is recounted in terms that emphasize the divergence of worldview and sense of relationship that separates Native American culture from that of the urban medical establishment. Medical personnel are conscientious and determined to do their best for Alfred. Unfortunately, "the best" is framed in terms of scientific control and technological overkill, rather than human relationships and the placement of illness and death within the context of communal and personal support. The initial response of the coworker who discovered him unconscious—to call 911—was not inappropriate, given what must have been the uncertainty of his physical and mental status. Without placing blame on those who were only fulfilling their socially assigned roles, one still can note that this call for help was followed almost automatically with resuscitation, internment in the city hospital, and a respirator. Procedures and machines take over the human crisis.

Efficiency Versus Empathy

One can be more critical of decisions made when "agitated" Alfred's first attempt to remove the tubes is followed not by psychological support, pastoral counseling, or the encouragement of friends and family to gather at the bedside, but by the more single-minded, and perhaps more simple agenda of ordering "a complete workup" to reach "a definitive diagnosis" and determine the "best" treatment plan. Efficiency takes over for empathy, as medical personnel struggle to meet their "obligation" under the only rubric their setting provides. Though Alfred's friends express his hostility to "the white man's hospital," the staff "refused to withdraw treatment." They seem fixed on the prospect that their medical expertise might possibly alleviate physical symptoms. They are not able to appreciate the patient's distress at suffering the aggressive and ineludible "treatment plan" the city hospital seemed bent on implementing.

With his circumstances so reduced, Alfred's prospects and options are appallingly limited. Not among them is a dignified and comforted death in familiar surroundings, or even in the presence of those who might help him come to terms with his illness and mortality, Native American identity and Vietnam experience, religious hope and final repentance. Any way you look at it, Alfred was doomed to die surrounded—but alone.

The hospital staff is finally persuaded not to pursue its original course with regard to Alfred when he is able "to free his hands" and pull out the tubes. Apparently his action is symbolic of free, if not fully informed, consent. Albert shortly dies, apparently still in the hospital. The solution to a case like Alfred's is not simple autonomy, nor a "right" to be "assisted" (with more technology) in his lonely choice of death. The solution is to ask, at a deeper level, how we as a society handle illness and death, what we expect of medicine, and how we can provide the networks of care and concern in the negotiation of life's passages, which may flourish more readily in Native American cultures than in those of big-city hospitals and fast-food restaurants. People want assurance of a "controlled" death because they fear being trapped by the system, lacking any meaningful say in their own life's finale, and deprived of solace from dear ones.

Beyond Raw Autonomy

In early 1996, the 2nd and 9th Circuit Courts decided no longer to bar physician-assisted suicide, allowing patients like Alfred to check out of the treatment rat race early. Hailed as a victory for autonomy, these decisions in fact reveal the poverty, not only of health-care resource allocation, but of our cultural practices while being ill and of offering physical and spiritual support to the dying. In an interview following the Circuit Court decisions, Michael Grodin, a professor of Law, Medicine, and Public Health at Boston University, commented, "I think we can talk about assisted suicide after we give people health insurance, access to hospice care, universal access to pain relief, and psychosupport systems so people don't kill themselves rather than be abandoned."[1]

This is not to say that life should always be sustained, no matter what its condition. Sometimes death is so near, the quality of life so low, or the burdens of further treatment so disproportionate to the benefits expected, that nonresistance to death is the most appropriate course. Two points on such decisions are important. First, refusal of life-sustaining treatment, even of an already-initiated measure like a respirator or feeding tube, is not the same as direct killing or suicide. This is a distinction which moral philosophy and theology have long upheld.

Though refusing useful treatment can be wrong, allowing a disease process to take its course without putting up a further fight can be right, when the prospects for significant relief are low. Although both direct killing and refusing or removing treatment result in death, there is more direct involvement of the agent in acts of killing, both in regard to his or her intention and in regard to the action that he or she takes. It is true that we should not hide our responsibility in decisions to permit death behind the characterization "indirect killing." Nonetheless, refusal of therapy does involve a more limited responsibility for death than when we directly take a life.

The key issue in Alfred's case, however, is not the

means to death, but the set of circumstances that make
death seem worth fighting for. Alfred apparently was
found unconscious well before his disease alone would
have thrust him into that condition. What Alfred had
suffered were not vastly debilitating or painful symptoms, but dreams of death and fear of white men's cures.
Though we have no reason to doubt that those who
practiced medicine on Alfred were committed and well-
intentioned, the ideals and standards under which they
labored mitigated against humane and holistic care with
his welfare as a person at its center. It is not enough to
focus moral and medical attention on prolongation of
life as such, or even on raw autonomy, exercised in the
absence of any real sense of communal concern and
interconnection. To give the staff caring for Alfred its
due, they debated the implications of his rejection of
tubes and reversed their decision to act aggressively on
his behalf. No doubt they too felt caught, with no satisfactory choices available. As a first step, the institution-
alized process of discernment probably needs to be more
collaborative, engaging the patient or a proxy decision
maker who can act on his interests. More important,
ways to deal with Alfred's illness with which he would
feel more comfortable than with doctors trained in
"Western medicine" should have been open to all
involved in determining Alfred's future.

From a Christian perspective, death is an enemy, but
not an absolute evil. Though brought into the world by
sin, death is now part of the human condition. On
death's other side lies resurrection life. Yet the long history of health-care ministries sponsored by religious
congregations and churches testifies to the Christian
commitment to alleviate human suffering and save
human beings from premature or miserable decline.
This nuanced Christian understanding of death does not
dictate in any simple way how and when we accept

death, fight it courageously, or take action to hasten its arrival. Appropriate action in the concrete must be shaped by distinctive Christian values and virtues, nuanced to the demands and opportunities of particular situations.

Solidarity with Those Who Suffer

Solidarity is a key and most characteristic Christian value, deriving from Jesus' announcement of the "kingdom of God" and of the formation of the early community of faith around mutual love and unity (symbolized by Paul as the Body of Christ). Solidarity is built on natural human interdependence, transformed by compassion and mutual service. While freedom too is a Christian value, the New Testament portrays disciples as freed *from* sin *for* love of God and neighbor, not as granted a context-free autonomy to do as they will. Christian decisions about death in a medical context should be guided by respect for the inestimable value of life, realism about the inevitability of death, hope in resurrection life, and solidarity with our fellow human beings as they face this momentous event. The Christian stance toward suffering refrains from attributing it in all its forms to the will of God, and takes responsibility for reducing it. Although the course of life and death is not completely under human control, there is a place for the responsible exercise of human agency, a place limited by the boundary between faithful acceptance of the death of the sick and arrogation of the right to kill.

The first line of Christian action in the face of physical affliction is to be in solidarity with those who suffer. Solidarity is not merely a recognition of the freedom of others to act as they choose, in the hope that they have the knowledge and resources to improve their lot. Solidarity is the kind of empathetic identification with the

other that results in service and even self-sacrifice. Sherrill House in Boston, a skilled nursing facility associated
with the Episcopal Archdiocese of Massachusetts,
espouses a "philosophy of care" based on "recognition
of each resident's life experiences, accomplishments,
interests, and personal beliefs" as "essential to quality
of life." Most important is the building of a community
in which residents, families, staff and volunteers "work
together as partners to enrich quality of life" for residents.[2]

In West Seattle, Washington, the Sisters of Providence
have restructured nursing-home care at Providence/
Mount Saint Vincent by creating "neighborhoods" within one nursing facility, in which residents are no longer
segregated by diagnosis, prognosis, or level of care needed. Each wing accommodates 20 to 25 residents and has
been renovated to look more homelike, with a kitchen,
dining room, sitting room, laundry, and bedrooms.
Nursing home administrators "want to do away with a
model of care that they believe strips people of control
over their lives and thereby takes away their dignity.
They are striving for a system of care that places residents' needs above regulation and bureaucracy."[3] An on-
site day-care center keeps employees' children close to
parents, while allowing elderly residents the chance to
enjoy visits from youngsters. One woman, who came to
the facility with bone cancer and a predicted two days to
live, survived for two years, with much improved
health. She immersed herself in classes on current
events, exercise classes, and a book group, and began to
play the piano for the first time in seventy years.

One of the first neighborhood directors acknowledged
staff anxiety and confusion while moving to the new
model of care. However, she asserted, "When you talk
about dignity, being known and having preferences honored is a big part of that. The transition to resident-

directed care is time consuming and messy, and it takes a great deal of creativity. You can't give everyone everything they need 100 percent of the time. But it's the most dignifying model imaginable."[4]

This kind of creativity, flexibility, and communal commitment to human dignity was just what our friend Alfred needed in order to live meaningfully and hopefully with his illness. Some Christian health-care providers are resisting the drive toward legalized euthanasia, not by insisting that every life be preserved as long as possible, but by supporting patient self-determination— through advance directives; offering hospice and other supportive care to patients and families; providing effective pain management; and offering a range of other special, spiritual, and pastoral care support services.[5]

Alfred's tragedy was not that he tried to kill himself (whether directly or only indirectly, we are not sure), and was unwarrantedly frustrated in his attainment of that goal. His tragedy was that the lack of an adequate support network in which to confront his failing health drove him to the brink of death. Moreover, when he had reached that point, those around him were able to respond only with a therapeutic assault he experienced as so violent that death was a welcome release. Even after they had registered the sincerity of Alfred's choice of death, the staff response was another human failure. Letting him go in the name of self-determination, they never realized that his choice was forced by the bleakness of the therapeutic prison in which they held him captive.

NOTES

1. Peter S. Canellos, "Supreme Court likely next stop for suicide aid cases," *Boston Globe*, April 4, 1996.
2. Sherrill House brochure, "The Caring Choice."
3. Sandy Gilfillan, "Shakin It Up: Providence/Mount St. Vincent Blends Skilled Care with Neighborhood Setting," *Catholic Health World*, April 1, 1996, p. 3.
4. Ibid., p. 5.
5. "Catholic Providers to Redouble Commitment to Care for the Dying," *Catholic Health World*, April 1, 1996, p. 2. The Catholic Health Association (St. Louis) has joined with five health systems to form Supportive Care of the Dying: A Coalition for Compassionate Care.

STUDY GUIDE

When does a patient's choice of withdrawal from life-saving or life-prolonging medical treatment equate to suicide? If a medical staff does not forcibly intervene, is that not a form of assisted suicide?

Lisa Sowle Cahill carefully distinguishes between refusing life-sustaining treatment and direct killing or suicide. Refusing treatment, and respecting the decision of those who refuse, is not the same as suicide or assisted suicide, since one has a more limited responsibility for prompting death. Cahill contends that the "assisted-suicide" movement is prompted not so much by the questionable claims of personal liberty (raw autonomy), but by our deficient institutional systems that do not provide personal, supportive health care and treatment. She calls for Christian resistance to legalized euthanasia by creating alternatives, such as universal access to better health care, hospices, and pain management, along with special pastoral-care services.

Bruce Hilton emphasizes the priority of patient autonomy and does not equate patient withdrawal from treatment with suicide. He explores the dilemma of determining what a patient wants when the person can no longer communicate to family or health-care professionals. He underscores the role of hospital ethics committees. At the heart of ethical decision making are patient autonomy, informed consent, and the weighing of the burdens of a proposed treatment (like pain and suffering) versus the benefits (such as chances for full recovery).

Items for Reflection

1. Cahill speaks of the desire for "controlled death" as a response to people's fear of being trapped by the system, where "efficiency takes over for empathy." Do you agree with her that terminally ill persons would not choose suicide if the environment were more supportive?

2. Do you agree or disagree with the statement that "we can talk about assisted suicide after we give people health insurance, access to hospice care, universal access to pain relief, and psychosupport systems, so people don't kill themselves rather than be abandoned"?

3. There is no mention of a Living Will or any other informed consent document in Alfred's case. What are the advantages and disadvantages of a Living Will and Medical Durable Power of Attorney (see Appendixes)?

4. Do you know of situations like the one Hilton described, in which someone insisted that a loved one be kept alive beyond reasonable expectations? How do you think an ethics committee should handle such a case?

5. Hilton contends that the patient's wishes should be the sole criterion on which the decision to withdraw treatment should be made. Why do you agree or disagree?

CHAPTER FOUR

Physician Provided Medication for Termination of Life

*Mark A. Duntley, Jr., &
Robert M. Veatch*

DIANE

Recently, the *New England Journal of Medicine* published a short piece signed by Timothy E. Quill, M.D., which evoked a flood of national commentary by physicians and ethicists. After describing "Diane" as a stable and intelligent person with an incurable illness, Dr. Quill recounts the circumstances under which he provided her with sufficient medication to terminate her life:

> It was extraordinarily important to Diane to maintain control of herself and her own dignity during the time remaining to her. . . . As a former director of a hospice program, I know how to use pain medicines to keep patients comfortable and lessen suffering. . . . She wanted no part of it. . . . She wanted to take her own life in the least painful way possible. . . . I thought this request made perfect sense . . . but also thought that it was out of the realm of currently accepted medical practice. . . . She was more than willing to protect me by participating in a superficial conversation about her insomnia. . . . It was clear that she was not despondent and that in fact she was making deep, personal connections with her

family and close friends. . . . I wrote the prescription
with an uneasy feeling about the boundaries I was
exploring—spiritual, legal, professional and personal. Yet
I also felt strongly that I was setting her free . . . to maintain dignity and control on her own terms until her
death.*

---

* *The New England Journal of Medicine,* March 7, 1991,
  p. 692.

Physician Provided Medication for Termination of Life

Mark A. Duntley, Jr.

Fred was eighty-eight years old and had been in a nursing home for three years. His health was failing, but he was not suffering from a terminal illness. Fred had become incontinent and unable to care for himself in any active fashion, but his mind was still sharp. Then one day, he decided that he wasn't going to eat or drink anything ever again; he wanted to die. Even though they brought his tray of food at every meal time, the nursing-home staff honored Fred's wishes and allowed him to refuse it. As his family watched his life ebb away, they felt some admiration that Fred possessed this kind of courage and determination. But during the seven long days before he died, they also wondered if it wouldn't have been better if the staff had been able to just give him pills to end his life.

Christians, who over the centuries have affirmed the sacred nature of human life as a gift from God, have almost uniformly rejected all forms of suicide since the time of Augustine.[1] Arguments against suicide based on biblical commandments, the individual's relationship to God, natural law, and the avoidance of suffering have held sway in theological writings and cultural practices. The moral aversion of Christians toward suicide has influenced our legal traditions as well.[2]

Assisted suicide also has been traditionally rejected by Christians. In my own state of Oregon, attempts to legalize physician-assisted suicide, such as the 1994 Death with Dignity Act, have been greeted with apprehension and hostility by many Christians. One Christian leader suggested that the Death with Dignity Act

really was "selling murder in the name of mercy."[3] The
Legislative Committee of Ecumenical Ministries of Oregon, the largest state ecumenical organization, also
opposed the Death with Dignity Act, asserting that it
"attempts to disrupt the natural season and time of
death."[4] Many Christian physicians, including former
Surgeon General C. Everett Koop, strongly oppose
assisted suicide. Koop states that for the terminal
patient, the last months of life are "the time for the doctor to be the patient's support, not his/her killer."[5] After
the Death with Dignity Act was passed by Oregon voters, a state-wide survey of the attitudes of Oregon physicians found that 65 percent of those physicians who
identified themselves as Christians indicated that they
"would not participate" in an assisted suicide if the con-
stitutionality of the law were upheld.[6] Compared with
their non-Christian colleagues, Christian doctors in
Oregon were almost twice as likely to reject involvement in assisted suicide.

Even though Christian theologians, authorities, and
physicians continue to voice their opposition to assisted
suicide, I think that the story of Dr. Timothy Quill and
Diane should cause us to rethink our categorical opposition. A careful analysis of their story suggests that we
must reconsider three important factors in order to fairly assess the morality of assisted suicide. First of all, we
need to understand the way modern medicine combats
death, even in the face of extended, debilitating, and
often painful illnesses. Second, we need to rediscover
the power and preeminence of mercy, and what that
means in the Christian context of care for the dying.
And finally, we need to question the modern "consumer" approach to the physician-patient relationship
and reaffirm the superiority of a "covenantal" approach
to that relationship. In the following pages, I will
explore these issues and suggest that, at least in some

situations, assisted suicide can be an experience of mercy and grace.

Fighting Death in the Era of Modern Medicine

> I think people are genuinely scared about what might happen to them. Not everybody is, but many people have [fear], particularly people who have witnessed hard deaths or who are in the throes of this kind of illness. And it must be a relief to come in and have somebody who will talk to you about that, who will acknowledge that it exists, and there is a real problem here.
>
> Timothy Quill[7]

Esther had just learned that her colon cancer, which she thought had been treated successfully a few years earlier, had instead apparently metastasized throughout her body. Her condition was now terminal, and she was told that additional surgery and other treatments to eliminate the cancer would be useless. Esther began to put her affairs in order and prepare for the eventuality of hospice care. But within only a few weeks, she was taken in an ambulance to the hospital with excruciating abdominal pain. An X-ray indicated a perforated bowel, and she was rushed to the operating room. She awoke to find that this potentially fatal episode had been remedied, but her long-term prognosis was still the same. She remained in institutional care until her death five months later.

As medical technology has progressed, more and more of us have seen people like Esther receive the "gift" of additional time. But even for those whose pain is controlled, we find all too often that these life-extending treatments give them time, but their quality of life is drastically diminished, followed by the kind of death they always dreaded. Still, aggressive treatment at the extremes of life continues. In the push to "fix" people, we seem to be willing to treat the ailing 80-year-old and the seriously compromised 22-week-old premature infant much as we would treat a generally healthy 20-year-old. Do-not-resuscitate (DNR) orders notwithstanding, aggressive medical treatment remains the predominant model, even as people approach death.[8] It is no wonder people tend to fear the modern dying process.

Death used to happen to people mostly at home, in a peaceful environment surrounded by family. Now, 80 percent of the time, it happens in an institution where a battle is being waged against disease, and people are surrounded by monitors and machines. In our heroic attempts to make life longer and better through medical means, we all too often sacrifice the opportunity for a good death. Esther's "emergency" could have been handled quite differently. Without surgical intervention, extensive infection would have brought death within a day or two. Aggressive pain control with morphine could have kept her comfortable during that time. But she was never given this option. Instead, she suffered a slow, unpleasant death.

Unlike Esther, Diane was given the choice, and she decided that after all she had been through, a 25 percent chance was not enough to justify the possible misery she would face. She asked Dr. Quill to see her not as a patient to save, but as a person to honor. Diane feared some things more than death, and Dr. Quill listened and understood.

As the boundaries of life are extended by modern medicine, and we are faced more frequently with the suffering involved in dying slowly from a terminal disease, we should begin to question whether preserving life and making someone as comfortable as possible are the primary principles that should guide us in care for the dying. Mercy may actually be more fundamental in many ways, especially for those who face the immense burdens of a compromised quality of life and unrelenting pain. As Christians in particular, we are called to emulate the mercy of God in our relations with those in need.[9] However, before we can bestow mercy, we must understand its context and essence, as presented to us in the scriptures.

Covenant, Mercy, and Compassion

> Diane taught me about the range of help I can provide if I know people well and if I allow them to say what they really want. She taught me about life, death, and honesty, and about taking charge and facing tragedy squarely when it strikes. She taught me that I can take small risks for people that I really know and care about.
>
> Timothy Quill[10]

The Christian scriptures offer important insights when considering merciful treatment, for in the Bible we learn that the meaning of mercy is inextricably tied to the complete relational commitment of a covenant.[11] Many early biblical accounts, including the stories of Noah, Abraham, and David, attest to this integral relationship of divine covenant and mercy. Later in the history of Israel, the prophets reminded the people that in spite of Israel's infidelity and God's punishment, God's covenant with them could not be broken. Human failures aside, mercy would always be available to Israel because of the covenantal guarantee of God's faithfulness.

God's mercy is likewise set forth as a model for human beings to follow, and the key to obtaining human mercy rests within the covenantal relations between persons. Throughout scripture, mercy is found within committed human relationships, a sign of deep friendship and devotion. It is also an essential part of the covenantal relationship with those who are helpless or dependent upon the community.

It is, however, in the example of Jesus Christ himself that we find the key to a deeper understanding of mercy. For in the accounts of Jesus we find his covenantal relationships and acts of mercy linked through his deep compassion[12] for others. It is his complete commitment to others and his resulting ability to "suffer with" others that enables Jesus to heal the blind, feed the multitudes, and even raise the dead.[13] And finally, it is Jesus' compassionate love for his people that leads him to his greatest act of mercy on the cross at Golgotha. Thus, we find that in the life of Jesus the presence of mercy is a certain sign of deep compassion, developed within covenantal relationships.[14]

One of the most serious problems we face with modern medicine today is that precisely when we most need these covenantal relationships with our physicians—at the end of life—is also when we find out how infrequent they are. Instead of being healed, we are treated; instead of being a person, we are a case; instead of someone who is dying, we are someone with a terminal disease. We are consumers, and physicians are providers; our care is managed, and our relationships are contractual in nature. Yet, in order to truly dispense and receive mercy, a covenantal context must exist. Otherwise, we can only guess about whether real mercy is being offered.

Covenantal Relationships and Assisted Suicide

When you witness a hard death, it changes you in a fundamental way. You no longer see this as a simple issue.

You can't say it's simple, doctors should never get
involved in this, because it's so compelling and terrifying.

Timothy Quill[15]

Tom's ALS had progressed rapidly in the past year.
While leaving the mind intact, Amyotrophic Lateral
Sclerosis attacks the nervous system and eventually
destroys the muscular control throughout the entire
body. Death is inevitable, and there is no cure for the
disease. Tom had gone from walking to a wheelchair,
and at the age of thirty, he no longer could move his
arms and legs. His neurologist informed him that he
would soon require a feeding tube and respirator, since
he wouldn't be able to swallow or breathe for himself.
The neurologist did suggest hospice care, but the
thought of dying inch-by-inch in hospice care horrified
Tom. He had suffered enough and wanted to be free
from his disease. No longer able to write and barely able
to talk, Tom contacted Dr. Jack Kevorkian, who agreed
to help him end his life. Not long after that, Tom died in
the back of Dr. Kevorkian's Volkswagen van.

Unfortunately, it seems that, in this case, real mercy
was not offered to Tom either by his neurologist or by
Dr. Kevorkian. The neurologist was not able to see
Tom's inner fears of a horrible death, and instead,
focused his efforts on palliative care. In fact, they had
never even discussed suicide, and the neurologist
seemed puzzled by Tom's ultimate choice. And while
Dr. Kevorkian sensed Tom's anguish, and they had
talked briefly about assisted suicide, Dr. Kevorkian
never really questioned the appropriateness of Tom's
decision. He simply assumed that giving Tom what he
asked for would be merciful.

Apparently, neither the neurologist nor Dr. Kevorkian

fully understood the essence of mercy that Jesus mod-
eled. Mercy is not simply giving something you think a
person needs, nor is it simply giving something a person
says they want. Mercy is not about accepted standards
of care or about autonomy; it is an act that flows from a
deeply felt compassion. Neither physician demonstrated
a capacity for "suffering with" Tom in his anguish over
losing his life to ALS. While both of them thought they
knew what was merciful for Tom, their notions were
based on their own understandings, not on Tom's. Each
had a recipe for mercy that lacked the central ingredient
of compassion. In his process of dying, Tom needed a
doctor who could help him care not only for his body,
but for his soul. He needed a doctor who could talk to
him openly about dying, in an attempt to understand
him. Tom needed a doctor like Dr. Timothy Quill.

If we appropriate the life of Jesus as being paradigmatic for our own relationships, then we can argue that
developing compassion for others in the context of
covenantal relationships is a prerequisite for showing
mercy. Ultimately, Tom could not find mercy at the
hands of either doctor bcause he did not share a
covenantal relationship with either. Without this kind
of relationship, they were not able to develop true compassion for Tom. In contrast, Dr. Quill's own accounts
show that he was committed to Diane at an emotional,
intellectual, and spiritual level. Dr. Quill and Diane had
a relationship that was both professional and personal. It
was mutually enriching, and they understood each other
as friends and partners in a shared endeavor. Their relationship embodied the biblical model of covenant, and
Dr. Quill's compassion for Diane enabled him to understand how to show her mercy. In spite of any reserva-
tions we might have as Christians, it is precisely this
kind of covenantal context in which assisted suicide can
indeed become an experience of God's grace and mercy.

CONCLUSIONS

My view is that this ought to be an agonizing decision for a physician. This is only the last resort, after you've really thought about it and explored every other avenue. And it takes time, and it takes expertise.[16]

What should Christians say about assisted suicide? Is it right, or is it wrong? I believe that the most reflective Christian answer about the morality of assisted suicide is that "it depends." There are cases where assisted suicide is wrong, and there are also cases where assisted suicide is right. But how can we tell which are which? Unfortunately, no sophistication with moral principles or precision about the consequences of our actions will provide us with the criteria. For the true task of Christian ethics lies not in identifying normative principles or creating the best consequences, but rather in understanding what is going on and what response will "fit" into what God is doing.[17]

The only way we can be sure we are not missing the mark concerning assisted suicide is to get beyond merely saying no. In order to accomplish this, we must dedicate ourselves to being open to the whole picture—to examining the entire breadth of the moral landscape and seeing its intricate complexities. In addition, we need to understand that in prolonging life, modern medicine has changed forever the way we die. We need to rediscover that mercy should lie at the heart of how we care for the dying. We need to question the norm of contractual relationships between physicians and patients, and come to see that mercy cannot be certain without covenantal relationships which nurture our ability to feel compassion. Then we can move beyond the simple rejection of assisted suicide and begin to watch with open spirits for those times when merciful care for dying persons involves helping them to die. When we do all this, we will find more situations like Diane's, where assisted suicide can indeed be a Christian moral response to the question, "How shall we die?"

NOTES

1. Augustine was the first significant Christian theologian to condemn suicide. See *Concerning the City of God Against the Pagans*, trans. Henry Bettenson (Harmondsworth: Penguin, 1984), Book I, Chapter 20.
2. Margaret Pabst Battin, *Ethical Issues in Suicide* (Englewood Cliffs, N. J.: Prentice Hall, 1995), pp. 17-57.
3. Archbishop William Levada, "Measure 16 violates solemn obligation to protect weak," *Catholic Sentinel*, September 2, 1994, pp. 5, 17.
4. *Oregon Official 1994 General Election Voters' Pamphlet*, p. 131.
5. Ibid., p. 127.
6. Melinda Lee, et al., "Legalizing Assisted Suicide-Views of Physicians in Oregon," *The New England Journal of Medicine*, (February 1, 1996), pp. 310-15.
7. Frontline, "The Kevorkian File." Public Broadcasting Service, April 5, 1994.
8. See "A Controlled Trial to Improve Care for Seriously Ill Hospitalized Patients," *Journal of the American Medical Association*, November 22/29, 1995, pp. 1591-98; Bernard Lo, editorial, "Improving Care Near the End of Life. Why is it so Hard?" *Journal of the American Medical Association*, pp. 1634-36.
9. The parable of the "Good Samaritan" in Luke 10:25-37 is a paradigmatic example.
10. Timothy E. Quill, "Death and Dignity: A Case of

Individualized Decision Making," *New England Journal of Medicine*, March 7, 1991, p. 694.

11. Although the concept of covenant is by no means uniform throughout scripture, one of its central meanings is the presence of a complete, personal commitment to another.

12. The word "compassion" comes from the Latin root *com passus*, which, literally translated, means to "suffer with."

13. His inner feelings of compassion (*splagchnizomai*, literally "to be moved in one's bowels") prompt Jesus to act with mercy (*eleeo*). See Matt. 20:29-34; Mark 1:40-42; Mark 6:34-44 and Luke 7:11-15. See also the parable of the unforgiving servant in Matt. 18:23-35.

14. For a more complete discussion of covenant, compassion, and mercy, see George Mendenhall, "Covenant" in *The Interpreter's Dictionary of the Bible* (Nashville: Abingdon Press, 1962), Vol. 1, pp. 714-23, and Elizabeth Achtemeier, "Mercy" in Vol. 3, pp. 352-54.

15. *Frontline*, "The Kevorkian File," Public Broadcasting Service, April 5, 1994.

16. Ibid.

17. I refer here to "Responsibility Ethics." See H. Richard Niebuhr, *The Responsible Self* (New York: Harper, 1963).

Physician Provided Medication for Termination of Life

Robert M. Veatch

Timothy Quill is often viewed by defenders of physician-assisted suicide as the answer to Jack Kevorkian. If Kevorkian represents the worst of physician assistance—crude, make-shift technology for patients who are virtual strangers, performed by a former pathologist untrained in the skills of psychological assessment and no longer licensed to practice medicine—Timothy Quill is often viewed as a much more plausible role model. He describes a patient known and counseled over a prolonged period by a caring, compassionate physician, who practices in a well-respected medical center and has struggled to convince his patient to pursue palliative alternatives in which he is skilled.[1] He is cited by advocates of voluntary physician-assisted suicide who cringe in embarrassment at Kevorkian.

Reasons for Supporting Quill

The reasons to support Quill are, by now, well-known by medical ethicists.[2] His patient's suffering, mental and physical, probably will be minimized. Even comparing it with a decision to forgo life-support and adopt a palliative, hospice approach, it is quite possible that her suffering would be less with a quick, painless, medically efficient, professionally informed death by barbiturates. Moreover, assuming that suicide and forgoing treatment are other options available to her, she will be dead soon in any case. The "sacredness of life" concern will be defeated, no matter what. These points raised by Quill's supporters are concerns that must be taken seriously, but miss much of the complexity of Quill's decision.

The Standard Critique of Physician-assisted Suicide

The standard arguments against physician assistance in suicide are also to be taken seriously.[3] They have been with us for centuries and, until very recently, were almost universally accepted in matters of law and ethics.

The Slippery Slope's Newfound Grease

First, critics of active killing, including physician-assisted suicide such as that of Quill, offer what is often called the "wedge," or slippery-slope argument.[4] It is favored by utilitarians as a rebuttal against the claim that more good will be done if active merciful killing, including suicide, is condoned. If killings are condoned out of mercy, especially in cases that do not involve aggressors against the interests of others, eventually, so the argument goes, society will become accustomed to such killings. Killings will become easier and more tolerable psychologically. Innocent life will be taken in more and more cases, including those in which the patient has not requested to be killed, or even those in which the patient is not yet ready to die. If we can judge killing by the consequences, the innocent will die unnecessarily. Worse still, those who are a drain on society could justifiably be done away with. Although the claim is controversial, some say this is what happened in Nazi Germany, and they fear it could happen elsewhere.

The argument used to be speculative. Comparing the envisioned benefit to the suffering terminally ill, such as Diane, with the hypothetical loss of life of innocent people who did not request killing led to enormous differences in estimates of whether permitting physicians to assist in death, on balance, would really do more good or harm.

But now we have another cultural laboratory. The Netherlands, for several years, had a policy of tolerating physician assistance in death for terminally ill patients who persistently and voluntarily ask their physicians for help. Technically, to this day, it is not legal for physicians to assist through mercy killing, but a widely publicized agreement exists between the profession and public authorities not to prosecute, provided proper procedures were followed (including the important requirement that the assistance take place only after persistent and voluntary requests from a competent patient, a condition apparently met in Timothy Quill's case).

A governmental commission produced a report, the Remmelink Report, attempting to assess the effects of this quasi-legalization of physician assistance in dying.[5] The result was startling. Using three different methods of determining the effects, the investigators estimated that during the period under study, there were 2,318 cases of physician assistance in death, following the terms of the agreement. Whether this number is large or small is hard to say; it probably depends upon one's general attitude toward the practice of euthanasia. Regardless, the commission also found that during the same period, an additional 1,030 life-terminating acts took place *without* an explicit and persistent request. This figure does not include an additional huge number of deaths from narcotic respiratory depression (some 17% of all deaths occurring in the country), a kind of active intervention that "indirectly" produces death that is legal and ethically acceptable, in both the United States and the Netherlands. The thousand deaths were cases in which physicians admitted to administering lethal agents for the purpose of killing patients who had *not* persistently and voluntarily requested to be killed.

It seems overwhelmingly clear that the shift in cultural attitude that surrounds the quasi-legalization of physician assistance in euthanasia after persistent and voluntary requests has created a climate of tolerance for other details that do not involve voluntary requests or in which the requests are not persistent. To have a thousand people caught in that climate who do not fit the conditions seems like an enormous spillover from the 2,318 deaths that the policy intended to cover. Some of these were the senile elderly; others, isolated persons who were a burden to society; still others, infants and children. Some very well may have been competent patients who were simply never asked. Most of them could have ended their lives legally and ethically by forgoing life-support—in a manner more carefully monitorable by the health professional community and the public.

In many ways, the Quill case—because it is so much cleaner, more plausible, and more ideal—is much more dangerous than that of Jack Kevorkian's patients.[6] While Kevorkian has generated skepticism and hostility, Quill's efforts, seemingly more credible, have brought sympathy. A grand jury refused to indict, even though he confessed to a crime publicly in a widely read medical journal.

The Remaining Power of the
Sacredness-of-Life Argument

The second traditional argument against physician assistance in death is also well-rehearsed. Critics insist that the appeal to the sacredness of life, or as it sometimes is expressed more precisely, the principle of avoidance of killing, really does survive as a fundamental moral belief. These critics argue that there is something precious about every human life which requires that humans never intentionally act to destroy it. They attempt to hold on to the difference between intended killing, which they deem unacceptable, and the more carefully formulated notion of forgoing disproportionately burdensome life support, which has been deemed acceptable within both Christian and secular thought for centuries, going back to the days of Thomas Aquinas. Some ground that prohibition in religious language—that human life is created by God and not to be subject to human fallible decision.

It is a mistake, however, to view this prohibition against killing as exclusively a religious principle. Secular philosophers have reached very similar conclusions. Immanuel Kant, for example, insisted that the human life always be treated as an end in itself and never as a means only. He held that doing so led to a prohibition on killing. Others have reached similar conclusions, at least insofar as the life is innocent. Catholic theologians, led by Cardinal Joseph Bernardin, have recently developed the "seamless garment" argument, holding that if Catholics are to take seriously that life is sacred, then they must view all life in that way—having implications for mercy killing, war, and efforts to save the lives of the poor, as well as for the abortion debate.[7] Many Protestants also find such preciousness in human life that they feel it never should be intentionally destroyed.

Incompatibility with the Healing Role

There is a third concern of those who oppose physician assistance in dying. They worry specifically about *physician* assistance. They recognize health professionals as playing a critical function—providing care and compassion in the form of healing and relief of suffering.[8] Of all roles, they see the health professional as committed to doing what is possible to heal. That, they feel, is incompatible with making the health professional a euthanizer (or even an assistant euthanizer).

It is not clear whether these more traditional arguments against physician participation in suicide, such as that of Timothy Quill, will persuade those who are not already convinced. Just as defenders of the more traditional norms need to take seriously the degree of suffering of people like Diane, so defenders of Timothy Quill need to give attention to a set of arguments that have survived centuries. What perhaps tips the balance are two newer arguments against Quill that raise problems, even for those of us who are not totally convinced by the power of the traditional antieuthanasia arguments.

New Arguments Against Physician-Assisted Death

1. The Dangers of Insisting on Voluntariness

Defenders of physician assistance in suicide often rest their case in a form of liberalism which stresses that there is no harm and much good that can come from permitting people whose competence has been thoroughly assessed to voluntarily end their lives. Thus in the Netherlands, the critical feature of physician participation is that the patient's request be both voluntary and persistent. In the referenda attempted in Washington and California, and in the one passed in Oregon, significant provisions are made for assessment of patient mental status.[9] Kevorkian is criticized for his lack of provision of competent assessment of competence. On this ground, Quill has done fairly well. He at least had the benefit of contact over a prolonged period.

But what will be the consequences of limiting physician assistance to cases of demonstrated competence? A look at the medical situation today makes very clear that the real problem is the prolonged, sometimes tortuous treatment of children, the senile, and others who are not competent to make any medical decision on their own, much less to generate persistent, voluntary requests to be assisted in taking lethal medications. In some jurisdictions, including Missouri[10] and New York,[11] rulings still imply that family members do not have the legal authority to decide to forgo life support for incompetent patients who have not left clear and convincing evidence of their wishes.

We are at a critical point. As a society, we seem to have a choice between two strategies that move us in opposite directions. One approach would be to postpone any further discussion of voluntary active killing of a small number of competent people who want medical assistance in bringing about their deaths, until we have addressed the dilemma of patients who are incompetent to ask that life support be omitted. This requires recognizing that, in some cases, it is not patient choice, but patient burden that drives decisions by their surrogates to forgo life support. This approach downplays voluntary choice in order to protect the welfare of incompetents.

The other approach moves us diametrically in the opposite direction. It pushes voluntary choice to the center stage, making it the basis for expanding the present policy to include active mercy killing and assisted suicide, in cases in which competent patients have voluntarily asked to be killed.

The more the movement to legalize the assistance of physicians stresses that the voluntary choice of competent patients is the critical feature in legitimizing decisions, the more the group of incompetent patients is relegated to second-class patienthood, stranded in a land where no one is permitted to acknowledge the fruitlessness of life-supporting interventions. Diane's plight is a tragic one, but she has options: palliative care that will control physical suffering, suicide drawing on existing, widely disseminated literature from groups like the Hemlock Society, and even assistance in suicide from those outside medicine who are willing to circumvent the law in courageous fear and trembling. For example, in Washington, clergyman Ralph Mero is leading a group called Compassion in Dying that provides such assistance, even as the Washington law is being tested in the courts.[12] It is this group that was behind the recent United States Court of Appeals ruling in favor of the right of competent patients to obtain assistance in suicide.

The number of people who cannot be helped humanely by other, more traditional palliative methods is very small, compared to the number—in the thousands at any given time—who are stranded in a state of incompetence, suffering or permanently unconscious, waiting for a law to be clarified, so that their suspended subhuman lives can end. Only if we temporarily suspend the quest for the ultimate in self-determination in the small number of physician-assisted suicide cases, can our society stop to bring this much larger group the relief they need.

2. The Arrogance of Physician Assistance

Even if this newfound concern for the incompetent, the weakest, and most vulnerable among us does not provide sufficient reason to be skeptical of Timothy Quill's plunge into the role of hero, perhaps a more careful reflection on the character of physicians will. Not all opponents of physician-assisted suicide are doctrinaire, dogmatic opponents of euthanasia. Some are legitimately worried about the particular dangers of encouraging people in the role of physician to make irreversible, sometimes not-carefully-thought-out decisions that result in the death of another human being.

It is the nature of the personalities of many physicians that they are self-confident, sometimes to the point of arrogance. They are willing to confess to the world that they have flouted the law as if they were above it. It is the nature of the profession of medicine that sometimes this self-confident willingness to rush to judgment is necessary. When the emergency room physician faces an apparently lifeless, unconscious patient who is not breathing, it is necessary to have someone who, on his or her own, without the benefit of peer consultation or review of text, is willing to take a knife and slit a throat in order to establish an airway. Instantaneous, confident, bold decision making is, in that setting, a virtue that saves life. But when Timothy Quill or Jack Kevorkian, or the intern who confesses to killing a stranger patient named Debbie use that arrogance to bring about death, the risks are too great.[13]

There are certain roles in society that should not include unreviewed decisions that lead to death. Even for those who are willing to experiment cautiously with legalization of assisted-suicide or euthanasia, there is something to be said for keeping certain people out of this business. For example, even if euthanasia were legalized, there is something discomforting about an elementary schoolteacher moonlighting as a euthanizer. Even if she were perfectly skilled and never mixed her night work with that of her daytime, it should make us uncomfortable.

So likewise, the role of physician, as long as it attracts the personality traits it presently does, should be isolated from assisting in suicide. Physicians do not make good killers. Far better that the role of merciful killer be reserved for those with a more humble temperament and a more vivid awareness of human fallibility. Do we want life in the hands of a man so arrogant that he is willing to publicly confess to a crime resulting in his patient's death? I think not. Far better, if we are to legalize active assistance in suicide, that we authorize it from a profession far closer to the roots of morality and far more cognizant of human finitude—the clergy, for example.

NOTES

1. Timothy E. Quill, "Death and Dignity: A Case of Individualized Decision Making," *New England Journal of Medicine,* March 7, 1991, pp. 78-81.
2. James Rachels, "Active and Passive Euthanasia," *New England Journal of Medicine,* January 9, 1975, pp. 78-80.
3. Robert M. Veatch, *Death, Dying and the Biological Revolution,* Rev. Ed. (New Haven, Conn.: Yale University Press, 1989).
4. Tom L. Beauchamp, "A Reply to Rachels on Active and Passive Euthanasia," *Social Ethics: Morality and Social Policy,* ed. T. A. Mappes and J.S. Zembaty (New York: McGraw-Hill, 1977), pp. 67-75.
5. Paul J. Van der Maas; Johannes J. M. Van Delden; Loes Pijnenborg; and Casper W. N. Looman, "Euthanasia and Other Medical Decisions Concerned the End of Life," *The Lancet,* September 14, 1991), pp. 669-74.
6. Jack Kevorkian, *Prescription Medicide: The Goodness of Planned Death* (Buffalo, N. Y.: Prometheus Books, 1991).
7. Joseph Bernardin, "A Consistent Ethic of Life: An American-Catholic Dialogue," speech delivered on December 6, 1983, at Fordham University. See *The Seamless Garment,* pp. 3-8.
8. Willard Gaylin, Leon Kass, Edmund Pellegrino, and Mark Siegler, "Doctors Must Not Kill," *Journal of the American Medical Association,* April 8, 1988, pp. 2139-40.

9. "The Oregon Death with Dignity Act," *Ethical Issues in Death and Dying,* 2nd Ed., ed. Tom L. Beauchamp and Robert M. Veatch (Upper Saddle River, N. J.: Prentice-Hall, 1996), pp. 199-206.

10. Cruzan, by *Cruzan v. Harmon,* 760 S.W.3d 408 (Mo.banc 1988).

11. In re *Westchester County Medical Center on behalf of O'Connor,* 72 N.Y. 2d 517, N.E. 2d 607 (1988).

12. Lisa Belkin, "There's No Such Thing as a Simple Suicide," *The New York Times Magazine,* Nov. 14, 1993.

13. "It's Over Debbie," *Journal of the American Medical Association,* January 8, 1988, p. 272.

STUDY GUIDE

The highly publicized and controversial case of Dr. Timothy Quill, who assisted his patient, Diane, to die, prompts two distinctly different Christian responses from Mark A. Duntley, Jr., and Robert M. Veatch.

Duntley asserts that physician-assisted suicide, if experienced in a loving, caring, covenantal relationship between patient and physician, can be "an experience of God's grace and mercy." He calls Christians to rethink categorical opposition to all suicide, in light of contemporary aggressive medical treatment given even when quality of life is diminished and a dreaded process of death is inevitable. When asked whether assisted suicide is right or wrong, he says the reflective Christian should answer, "it depends" on the particular circumstances.

Veatch dissents from Quill's action, reminding readers of three standard arguments that almost universally have prevailed until recently. The "wedge" or "slippery slope" approach contends that society will become accustomed to physician-assisted killings, and the suicide numbers will increase. He also emphasizes the sacredness of human life, which never should be intentionally destroyed. It is incompatible for the medical professional to be both healer and euthanizer. Patients have other alternatives, rather than using physicians.

Items for Reflection

1. Discuss whether being merciful means being open to assisted suicide, or whether Archbishop Levada is correct in asserting that the euthanasia movement is "selling murder in the name of mercy."

2. How does Duntley's description of contemporary medical care and relationship correspond to the experiences you and your family have known?

3. Veatch argues that the current legal emphasis on the legitimacy of *voluntary* decision making about assisted suicide makes "second-class citizens" out of persons who cannot make voluntary requests—for example, persons in coma. How do you respond?

4. When you consider your own death or that of a loved one, can you imagine ever calling a Dr. Quill or a Dr. Kevorkian? Why?

CHAPTER FIVE

A Family Member Helps a Patient Stop Breathing

John B. Cobb, Jr., &
Richard A. McCormick, S.J.

William F. Meyer, Jr. drew his last breaths with his head encased in a plastic bag. It was an inelegant but expedient way to end his life, instead of succumbing slowly to the cancer that had begun in his colon and spread to his lungs.

" 'I happily decided that it was more kind and thoughtful of me to terminate my life before I reached a decadent condition of helplessness,' the 88-year-old Mr. Meyer wrote in a letter that he had photocopied, addressed, stamped, and left to be mailed to some 80 friends and relatives.

"Late last month, the same officers who had nodded sympathetically to the younger Mr. Meyer [65] when they read his father's farewell message, arrested him. After a magazine published Mr. Meyer's account of how he helped his father kill himself, he was charged with second-degree manslaughter. If convicted, he faces 10 years in prison."*

* *The New York Times*, October 28, 1994. *AllNews*, December 15, 1994, Hartford Courant reports that William F. Meyer III was placed on probation for two years for his role in the death of his father.

A Family Member Helps a Patient Stop Breathing

John B. Cobb, Jr.

I live in a retirement community composed of former churchworkers and their spouses. Perhaps half of them spent twenty or more years as missionaries in other countries. Others have been YMCA workers, pastors, and seminary professors. On a theoretical basis, there are differences among us about the right to die.

Dreading Long-Protracted Dying and Ceasing to Be

On the other hand, our attitudes and spontaneous responses are remarkably similar. We enjoy our life together, considering ourselves fortunate to live in a community in which there is so much vitality and so much mutual care. Most of us are in no hurry to die. At the same time, few fear death. What we do fear—perhaps dread is a better term—is long-protracted dying. Even more, we dread that long-protracted state of ceasing to be one's self, even when the body is not dying, as is the case with Alzheimer's.

Twice a month, on average, the death of one of our companions is announced to us. Very rarely is there any feeling of shock or distress. If the death has been abrupt and unexpected, we rejoice that the one who died was spared what we all dread. If the one who died has long been dying, or suffering from Alzheimer's, we express our great joy and relief that death has come. In short, although we love life and live it fully, death, the ancient enemy, has become a friend.

We wish that the medical profession, set up to fight the ancient enemy, could adjust to this change brought about by its almost miraculous achievements. We sign documents asking to be allowed to die when the time comes. "Cooperate with our friend," we beg. But we know how little effect this request usually has, how automatic are the efforts in the emergency room and on the operating table to add a few unwanted weeks or months or years to our lives.

If Only Doctors Could Help

We do not blame the doctors or the hospitals. All our lives, we have been grateful for their commitment to life and have benefited from it. Even now, we want good treatment to enable us to recover from minor sicknesses and accidents. We cannot specify in advance every circumstance under which we want treatment and every circumstance under which we want to be left alone. So we hope for the good fortune of dying easily and without medical intervention.

We hope also for the sympathetic understanding of our doctors, and even for their help. How good it would be if they could help us in making the difficult decision when it is time to die, and then assist us in implementing that decision! But that time has not yet come.

Those feelings come to me again as I read the story of William F. Meyer. How much better it would be if we lived in a society in which he could have consulted not only with family and friends but also with those who know best the prognosis of disease and treatment! How much better to have them help make the decision as to when it is best to terminate the painful and unrewarding. How good it would be if doctors could share with us their process, superior knowledge of the options, help us choose, and help us implement the choice. In such a world, there would, I feel sure, be better options than a plastic bag over the head.

But we do not live in that happier context. We must work out our decisions without much help from the medical profession. At a time when we are unlikely to be able to implement our decisions on our own, we are put in the position of asking help from those who lack expertise and are in a poor position to intervene. We also are asking them to take risks in our behalf. It is hard to say that we have the right to impose this burden on those we love. For this reason, many of us will choose to do nothing, to let the disease and treatment take their dreadful course.

An Act of Love, Not Sin

I do not say that the father was wrong to ask this help from his son. I do not know. But in responding to this story, I need to make my real uncertainty on this point clear. I do not think I would make the request, although if help were offered, I probably would accept with deepest gratitude.

But for the son who responded to his father's wishes at great personal cost, I feel admiration. He was willing to engage in a distasteful and difficult act for his father's sake. He was willing to break the law openly, risking the consequences of trial and imprisonment for himself, in order to release his father from protracted suffering. Greater love has no one than this—that one sacrifice oneself in this way for another.

Nevertheless, our society officially tells us that William Meyer III committed the crime of manslaughter, and many representatives of the Christian community tell us that his deed was sinful. The burden of proof, I think, is on them. On the surface, the New Testament tells us that we are to act out of love for God and neighbor, and this pair of commandments sums up and supersedes the many rules that may, under most circumstances, guide our expression of love. The New Testament does not encourage us to produce a new set of rules, which we would then treat as absolutes, even when they conflict with the expression of love. How then can a Christian call this act of love a sin?

There are many answers, and although I find none convincing, we must take them seriously. It can be argued in biblical terms, that the law of love does not supersede the Ten Commandments. In this view, the Ten Commandments tell us what is everywhere and always a correct expression of the law of love. Hence, the commandment not to kill can never be set aside under this law.

Understanding the Commandment Not to Kill

Whether it is possible to formulate verbally rules of action that everywhere and always are required by love has been debated by Christians for a long time. I belong to the group that believes we should not try to do this, although we certainly can come close. The commandment not to kill is one that comes close.

But if we claim that it comes close, we must look at it more closely. It is clear from its context that it never meant that under no circumstances should one take the life of another human being. In the laws most closely associated with the Ten Commandments, capital punishment was ordered for a variety of crimes. Few Hebrews or Jews have thought that war was forbidden. What was forbidden is better named "murder."

But murder is not carefully defined. Ordinarily, this creates no difficulty. When one person kills another in order to steal possessions or to avenge a real or supposed injury, we know that is murder. When one person kills another in self-defense, we think it is not. Hence, we must consider the circumstances and purposes carefully. The law in every land, including Israel, does this.

Of one thing we can be sure. In its original formulation, what was envisaged was not the case of a son helping a father to carry out the father's reasonable wishes. The argument that this is forbidden by the Ten Commandments requires extensive justification. I do not find it persuasive.

Historically, most of the argument against suicide and assisting in suicide has been derived from natural-law theory, rather than the Bible. Saint Thomas argued that whereas we are responsible for many things in our lives, our entry into life and our departure from it are, and should be, left in God's hands. In his day, that made sense. But if we had really avoided intervention in these matters, death would come much sooner for many of us. It would still be the enemy. It is precisely because we have intervened so much and so successfully that life has been protracted and death has become the welcomed friend. It is arbitrary at this late date to introduce a principle here that is applied nowhere else.

Most generally, the argument can be drawn from natural law that all our acts toward others should envisage their true good and that this requires their life. It is concluded that the maintenance of the life of the other is an absolute requirement, regardless of the preferences of the other. It is sometimes said that any other position demeans human dignity.

Taking Seriously Another's Desires

It is, however, equally possible, and I believe truer, to say that love expresses itself in taking seriously the other's desires and helping to implement them. Of course, there are times when we doubt the wisdom of the other's desires, and out of love and genuine concern for their well being, we act in a contrary way. This is especially true in relation to our children, but it can apply to people of any age. This could certainly mean that we would refuse to cooperate in another's death, out of the conviction that the judgments on the basis of which the other has chosen death are mistaken.

If the son in the present instance had reason to think his father exaggerated the misery in store for him or underestimated the prospects of a good life, love would express itself in trying to persuade his father to change his mind and, probably, in refusing cooperation. It is the assumption that this was not the case that leads me to judge the son's act favorably. But to suppose in general that greater respect would be shown for the father's dignity by refusing to support him in his decision expresses a strange and, I think, demeaning notion of human dignity. It is my hope that this notion will not govern the way I am dealt with by others as I grow older, but I know that this does happen often.

Life Beyond its Proper and Desired Terminus

There is another set of considerations that certainly must be taken seriously. There are actions which, while positive when taken in abstraction from the social context, are harmful in that context. It can be argued that taking one's own life, or helping another to do so, even for the relief of great suffering, is of this sort. The persons immediately involved benefit, but each such act erodes a necessary principle in society. The argument is that the subtle distinction between those rare cases in which cooperating in another's death has adequate justification, and the vastly greater number of instances in which it does not, cannot be formulated in either law or moral codes. To protect the many, the law must permit no exceptions, and morality requires the upholding of the law.

This argument would be valid if its premises were accurate. Until fairly recent times, no doubt, they were. But now the frequency with which life continues beyond its proper and desired terminus is such that we are dealing with a mass phenomenon. It is so pervasive that it is on the minds of all of us of advanced years who see what happens to our friends. It is a source of dread for most of us.

If we are told that it is selfish and sinful for us to ask for the right for help in dying when the time comes, because this would endanger the situation for others, we ask who those others are. We know that the vast expenditure on the elderly to keep us alive, often against our wishes, exhausts public resources that are then not available for public-health services for pregnant mothers and young children. And we wonder whether the risks involved in allowing the elderly to participate in decisions about when they will die, and to receive help in implementing such decisions, would do more harm than that.

Going Beyond the Risks of Accepting "Assisted Suicide"

Yes, there are risks in public acceptance of "assisted suicide." This means that new legislation needs to be formulated carefully, and then tested in practice. We need, in this process, the help of those who are most fearful of the results, since they will notice dangers that those of us who mo st hope to benefit from such legislation will not see. No matter how carefully we ensure that decisions involve all relevant parties, that they are made responsibly, and that the right to die is limited to those who truly have no prospects for a significant and satisfying future, there will be abuses. In that respect, this legislation is no different from any other. The leg-

islative task is to formulate laws that will reduce point-
less suffering, indignity, and misery as much as possible,
while minimizing negative consequences.

I accept, therefore, the general point that we must be
willing to make personal sacrifices for the common
good. I accept the point that this means that some
actions that are positive in isolation from the general
context must still be forbidden and punished. But when
the existing laws are so far from the desirable balance, it
is not wrong to violate them openly, so as to force public attention upon the suffering and injustice they cause.
On the contrary, this is an act of courage from which, in
time, many of us may benefit. It is a Christian and
moral act.

A Family Member Helps a Patient Stop Breathing

Richard A. McCormick, S.J.

One knows nothing of the relationship of the elderly Meyer to his son or to the eighty friends and relatives to whom he addressed his final letter. Were these relationships mutually caring and compassionate, characterized by shared values, perhaps even shared faith, and profound other-concern? Did his son and friends support him in his illness? Did they spend time with him? Did they see to it that he received adequate pain relief? We do not know. We can only guess. But the guess may not be totally arbitrary, for we do know one thing about William Meyer, Jr.: He viewed his own being in "a decadent condition of helplessness" as intolerable because he would be reduced to reliance upon others. Therefore, he saw his assisted suicide as being a "kind and thoughtful" act. Does this reflect a lack of trust in the others' compassionate care?

Cultural Context Promoting Assisted Suicide

Perhaps his statement does not tell us much about those relationships. But I think it does reveal a good deal about the cultural context in which Meyer did his inelegant dying. I am morally opposed to assisted suicide, whether by a physician or anyone else. And legalizing it would be a very dangerous folly. However important it may be to flesh out this moral and legal stance, I think it is much more important to examine the cultural factors that, together, lead many Americans, the Meyers included, to see the matter differently.

In this sense, the case of William F. Meyer, Jr., and his

son's indictment, is of less interest and concern to me than its cultural setting. I see seven components of this context, or setting; together, they could lure people into agreement with the Meyers.

1. The Denial of Mortality

Of course, it is impossible to deny mortality. But we can think and act in ways that contain implicit denials. Thus, writing of health care, Daniel Callahan noted:

> Our toughest problem is not that of a need to ration health care, though that will be necessary. It is that we have failed, in our understandable eagerness to vanquish illness and disability, to accept the implications of an insight available to all: We are bounded and finite beings, ineluctably subject to aging, decline, and death. We have tried to put that truth out of mind in designing a modern health-care system, one that wants to conquer all diseases and stay the hand of death.[1]

Thus, Callahan continues, "We have defined our unlimited hopes to transcend our mortality as our needs, and we have created a medical enterprise that engineers the transformation." The symptoms of this rejection of the fact of mortality abound.

Item: A wealthy society like ours must not allow anyone to die who can be saved. Witness the end-stage renal disease program of 1972, providing government-paid dialysis for all who need it. Indeed, a 1987 Harris poll revealed that most people (71% to 26%) believe that "health insurance should pay for any treatments that will save lives, even if it costs one million dollars to save a life."

Item: Intensive-care units are overused; too frequently they resemble high-tech hospices. As Joseph A. Califano, Jr., puts it: "A substantial number of patients admitted are elderly, in chronically poor health, with little chance for short-term survival."[2] Many patients are either too sick or not sick enough.

Item: Nearly 30 percent of Medicare's money goes to patients with less than a year to live. This figure has not varied appreciably in the last fifteen years.

Christopher F. Koller summarizes as follows: "Health care has much more important things to offer than the false hope of immortality."[3]

2. Absolutization of Autonomy

Until the last few decades, medicine was practiced in a highly paternalistic way. *Paternalism* refers to a system in which treatment decisions are made against the patient's preferences, or without the patient's knowledge and consent. The past twenty years have seen a reaction against paternalism and the flowering of patient autonomy.

What easily can be missed is that reactions have a way of becoming *over*reactions. In the religious sphere, a reaction against authoritarianism can usher in anarchy. In an overreaction against paternalism, autonomy has been absolutized. The symbolic cheerleader for this absolutization is Dr. Jack Kevorkian, who states:

> In my view the highest principle in medical ethics—in any kind of ethics—is personal autonomy, self-determination. What counts is what the patient wants and judges to be a benefit or a value in his or her own life. That's primary.[4]

The offshoot of this absolutization is that very little attention is given to the values that ought to guide the use of autonomy. The sheer fact that the choice is the patient's is viewed as the sole right-making characteristic of the choice. This attitude has impoverished the presentation of the pro-choice position on abortion.

Choices, however, may be good or bad, and unless we confront the features that make choices good or bad, autonomy usurps the evaluation. When it trumps every other consideration, autonomy has been overstated and distorted, and leads to what Bruce Jennings calls "the terrible singularity, the chilling aloofness of the sovereign moral will."[5]

3. Dignity as Independence

This is tied closely to the overstatement of autonomy. We often hear people, especially the elderly, declaring, "I don't want to be a burden." The idea of depending on others seems almost un-American. Depending on others is foreign to our notion of human dignity. Human dignity means independence, much as national dignity is anchored in the Declaration of Independence.

Obviously, I mean in no way to glamorize dependence. Our discomfort with dependence is quite understandable. But for too many people, dignity is *totally* incompatible with dependence. Thus dignity—as in death with dignity—means death in my way, at my time, by my hand.

All I would argue here is that our notion of dignity must incorporate the reality of dependence. Christians realize that Christ displayed great dignity in dependence: "Not my will but thine be done." Christians do not view dependence as depriving us of our dignity, but as a sacrament of our openness to and dependence upon God. In the fragility of dependence, we are invited to cling to trust in a power beyond our control. In this sense, a rejection of interdependence is closely tied to rejection of creaturehood and mortality. An Anglican study group showed real wisdom when it wrote:

> There is a movement of giving and receiving. At the beginning and at the end of life, receiving predominates

over and even excludes giving. But the value of human life does not depend only on its capacity to give. Love, *agape*, is the equal and unalterable regard for the value of other human beings, independent of their particular characteristics. It extends especially to the helpless and hopeless, to those who have no value in their own eyes and seemingly none for society. Such neighbour-love is costly and sacrificial. It is easily destroyed. In the giver it demands unlimited caring, in the recipient absolute trust. The question must be asked whether the practice of voluntary euthanasia is consistent with the fostering of such care and trust.[6]

Daniel Callahan has it exactly right when he notes:

It is a profound error to think we are somehow lessened as persons because dependency will happen to us, as if that condition itself *necessarily* robbed us of some crucial part of the self. It does not. There is a valuable and necessary grace in the capacity to be dependent upon others, to be open to their solicitude, to be willing to lean upon their strength and compassion. To be a self is to live with the perpetual tension of dependence and independence. The former is as much a part of us as the latter. The latter may just feel better, and surely flatters us more. It still remains only half the story of our lives, however.[7]

Clearly, the Meyers did not view things in this way.

4. *The Interventionist Mentality*

Corporately, we Americans are *homo technologicus.* We believe that the best solution to the dilemmas created by technology is more technology. Thus, Glennon Hospital in St. Louis spends $400,000 to treat lead poisoning, rather than attempting to correct the problems in the homes where lead poisoning originates. We use pesticides and discover only later that they are carcinogens. We tend to eliminate the maladapted condition (disabled, retarded, etc.) rather than adjust the environment to it.

The high-water mark of the interventionist mentality was the declaration of the late Joseph Fletcher that "laboratory reproduction is radically human, compared to conception by ordinary heterosexual intercourse."[8] The surest symptom that something is awry here is that the fun has gone out of things. Leon R. Kass puts it as follows:

> Against the background of enormous medical success, terminal illness and incurable disease appear as failures and as affronts to human pride. We refuse to be caught resourceless. Thus, having adopted a largely technical approach to human life . . . we now are willing to contemplate a final technical solution for the evil of human finitude and for our own technical (but unavoidable) "failure," as well as for the degradations of life that are the unintended consequences of our technical successes. This is dangerous folly. People who care for autonomy and human dignity should try rather to reverse this dehumanization of the last stages of life, instead of giving dehumanization its final triumph.[9]

5. Morality as Purely Personal

We often hear such declarations as: "It is not my concern what another does." "Each person must decide for him or herself." "Who am I to determine another's morals?" Or again, "I do not myself accept abortion, but I do not want to impose my morality on others." Such statements spring from a lonely individualism that supposes that you and I are islands, individual and isolated from the society and atomized within it.

One of the major mischiefs of this individualism is our failure to see the social dimension of many problems (physician-assisted suicide, abortion, reproductive technologies, human sexuality). A view of abortion as a matter of individual choice, for example, divides people, while abortion seen as a social problem could bring people together. Nearly everyone would agree that the conditions that lead to abortion (poverty, lack of education, broken families, lack of recreational alternatives, and so on) should be corrected.

Or again, sexual activity is often viewed as a purely private matter. Robert McAfee Brown recently underlined how false that view is.[10] Sexual relationships are microcosms of society. A loving atmosphere in the home can flow out into society. An inhumane and violent social atmosphere can turn on the family and shatter it. Sexual and social issues are inseparable. Or better, sexual issues are social issues.

6. Functional Assessment of the Person

I believe it is safe to say that many Americans unwittingly operate from a rather crude utilitarianism in many of their moral judgments. "If it produces good results, what can be wrong with it?" This bias toward producing results will naturally lead to an evaluation of people as producers. They will be regarded, supported, protected, in terms of their functionality or value to society. If that is the silently operating criterion, it is clear who will suffer.

7. The Nutrition-Hydration Debate

Several prominent cases (such as those involving Paul Brophy in Massachusetts and Clarence Herbert in California) have propelled this problem onto center stage. This was especially true in the Nancy Cruzan case. People can now be maintained in a persistent vegetative state for years, by use of nasogastric tubes or gastrostomy tubes. But must, or ought we do so? Few would argue for doing so when the patient has expressly declined such treatment while competent. But what about those who have not so expressed themselves? Here controversy has swirled around cases like that of Nancy Cruzan. Many ethicists and physicians are convinced that artificial nutrition and hydration are not required for persons diagnosed as irreversibly in a persistent vegetative state. They base this view on the judgment that continuing in a persistent vegetative state is not a benefit to the patient, and therefore is not in the patient's best interests. This is my own conviction, and I wrote as much in support of the Cruzans' decision to stop Nancy's gastrostomy feedings.

Others, however—a minority, I believe—view this decision in much more sinister terms. For example, some saw continuance in a persistent vegetative state as a "great benefit" to Nancy Cruzan. A group of authors writing in *Issues of Law and Medicine,* in 1987, stated: "In our judgment, feeding such [permanently unconscious] patients and providing them with fluids by means of tubes is not useless in the strict sense, because it does bring to these patients a great benefit—namely, the preservation of their lives."[11]

The most recent statement espousing this view comes from Bishop John H. Myers of Peoria, Illinois, in his pastoral instructions to health-care administrators. He argues that artificial nutrition-hydration efforts are not useless, since they "effectively deliver nutrients" to these patients, even though they do not reverse their vegetative state. To me, that judgment defines usefulness to the patient so narrowly that personal benefit is reduced to the maintenance of physiological functioning. Patient benefit is exhaustively defined by medical effectiveness alone. Daniel Callahan calls the outcome of this reasoning "as clear a case of slavery to technology as can be found."[12] Other authors (such as Gilbert

Meilander of Oberlin) view the cessation of artificial nutrition-hydration from persistent vegetative state patients as direct killing.

I cannot argue the case further here. My purpose is to note that the overwhelming majority of people I have polled on this matter do not want to be maintained indefinitely in a persistent vegetative state because they do not regard this as a benefit to them. Indeed, they are appalled at the prospect. This is the second thing (pain being the first) people fear about dying: the needless, heedless, and aimless (as they see it) prolongation of the process. Marcia Angell, executive editor of *The New England Journal of Medicine*, referred to "the tragic irony of our technological successes." She concludes that "some people now fear living more than dying because they dread becoming prisoners of technology."[13] And this is where the nutrition-hydration question directly touches the issue of physician-assisted suicide. If our public policies are going to mandate nutrition-hydration treatments and prevent the discontinuance of them, people will easily view physician-assisted suicide as a preferable alternative. I am compelled to note here that certain fanatical fringes of the pro-life movement are counterproductive. By saying that Nancy Cruzan was "starved" and "killed," they will drive people to embrace physician-assisted suicide.

Distinguishing Between Killing and Allowing to Die

Closely connected with the nutrition-hydration discussion, indeed a part of it, is the distinction betwen killing and allowing to die. I realize that certain instances of allowing to die are irresponsible (and equivalent to killing); in some cases the distinction is hard to apply persuasively. But the distinction has served us well for many decades, and it would be irresponsible to abandon it. Yet it is being fudged, not least by some courts that threaten with murder charges those who withdraw hopeless and dying patients from ventilators or other life supports.

Judge Robert Muir did this at one point in the Karen Quinlan case. Those who removed Karen from the respirator, he said, would be subject to New Jersey's homicide laws. When judges confuse the removal of life supports with homicide, they make homicide look all the more acceptable. One way to soften resistance to the unacceptable is to confuse it with the acceptable.

This was done by the United States Court of Appeals for the Ninth Circuit on March 6, 1996. It quite cavalierly collapsed and dismissed some rather standard distinctions (e.g., omission vs. commission; killing vs. administering pain-killers that could hasten death).

Decisions and policies do not exist in a vacuum. They bear the stamp of the time and culture that supports them. That William F. Meyer, Jr., could regard his assisted suicide as an act of kindness to family and friends, that his son could view his participation in it as an act of compassion is, I believe, a product of the seven cultural distortions I have listed.

NOTES

1. Daniel Callahan, *What Kind of Life: The Limits of Medical Progress* (New York: Simon & Shuster, 1990), p. 23.
2. Joseph A. Califano, Jr., *America's Health Care Revolution: Who Lives? Who Dies? Who Pays?* (New York: Random House, 1986), p. 104.
3. Christopher F. Koller, "Health Care Priorities: Four Things to Keep in Mind," *Commonweal*, April 23, 1993, p. 6.
4. *Free Inquiry* Interview, "Medicide: The Goodness of Planned Death," Fall 1991, p. 14.
5. Bruce Jennings, "Active Euthanasia and Forgoing Life-sustaining Treatment: Can We Hold the Line?" *Journal of Pain and Symptom Management*, July 1991, p. 316.
6. General Synod Board of Social Responsibility, Church of England, *On Dying Well* (London: Church Information Office, 1975), p. 22.
7. Daniel Callahan, *The Troubled Dream of Life* (New York: Simon & Schuster, 1993), p. 144.
8. Joseph Fletcher, "Ethical Aspects of Genetic Controls: Designed Genetic Changes in Man," *New England Journal of Medicine*, September 30, 1971, p. 781.
9. Leon R. Kass, "Death with Dignity and the Sanctity of Life," *Commentary*, March 1990, p. 43.
10. Richard Scheinin, "Love, Justice, Sex: These Three," *San Jose Mercury News*, October 31, 1992.

11. William E. May et al., "Feeding and Hydrating the Permanently Unconscious and Other Vulnerable Persons," *Issues in Law and Medicine*, 1987, pp. 203-11.
12. Callahan, *The Troubled Dream of Life*, p. 70.
13. Marcia Angell, "Prisoners of Technology: The Case of Nancy Cruzan," *New England Journal of Medicine*, April 26, 1990, p. 1228.

STUDY GUIDE

When a family member helps a parent commit suicide, prevailing laws call it a crime, and the church traditionally has labeled the action a sin.

John B. Cobb, Jr., however, suggests that it could be an admirable Christian and moral act, because it forces public attention on suffering and injustice and may in time be of benefit to others. He wishes medical doctors could help make decisions and create "better options than a plastic bag over the head." Love of neighbor, articulated by Jesus, however, must prevail over strict adherence to the commandment "you shall not murder." Cobb notes that people do not fear death, but dread long-protracted dying, and the "state of ceasing to be one's self, even when the body is not dying, as is the case with Alzheimer's." The medical extension of life negates the old argument that only God controls the length of our days.

Richard A. McCormick, S.J., morally opposes assisted suicide, whether by a physician or anyone else. In the case under consideration, he wondered whether the request for family-assisted suicide reflected problematic care that the family and friends might provide. What most concerns McCormick are the cultural distortions which seem to be prompting more acceptance of assisted suicide. Utilitarian ethical thinking and the absolutization of personal autonomy ignore society's interests and needs. The distinction between deliberately killing and allowing a person to die must be maintained. People should not be slaves to pain and the needless vegetative prolongation of life. Legalization of assisted suicide, however, would be a dangerous folly.

Items for Reflection

1. Do you agree with the respondents to a poll who replied that "health insurance should pay for any treatments that will save lives, even if it costs one million dollars to save a life"?

2. McCormick suggests that Christians should not seek to remain totally independent. "Our notion of dignity must incorporate the reality of dependence. . . . Christians do not view dependence as depriving us of our dignity, but as a sacrament of our openness to and dependence on God." Think of some situations in which you believe it is right for patients to be dependent upon others. Are there situations in which it is not justifiable? Is it an intended lesson of life that we experience the dependence of diminishment? Explain.

3. When commenting on a father's request that his son assist him in suicide, Cobb says, "I do not think I would make the request, although if help were offered, I would probably accept with deepest gratitude." If you were the father in this case, would you hestitate to ask? Do you think a son or daughter should volunteer to help, rather than waiting to be asked?

4. How do you feel about Cobb's perception that people don't fear death, but dread long-protracted dying and "ceasing to be one's self when the body is not dying," as happens with Alzheimer's?

CHAPTER SIX

A Couple's Joint Suicide

Joretta L. Marshall &
J. Philip Wogaman

ICHARD AND HELEN BROWN
"The day Richard and Helen Brown were
found dead in their garage, letters of explana-
tion began arriving in their friends' mailboxes.

"The ailing, elderly couple had chosen suicide so they could leave their $10 million fortune to
charity, rather than spend some of it on medical treatment.

" 'They were taking the high road to death,' their former pastor, Charles Heuser, of Gold Beach, Ore., said
Monday.

"In recent months, Richard Brown, 79, had to use a
wheelchair because of arthritis and asthma. Helen
Brown, 76, had Alzheimer's disease.

"The Browns' bodies were found Dec. 5 in their car in
the garage of their Fort Lauderdale, Fla., home. Both died
of carbon monoxide poisoning.

"Their wills specified that their money should go to
United Church of Christ organizations.

" 'We have the means to afford the best doctors, hospitals, and around-the-clock home care to the end of our
lives, but neither of us wants that kind of life,' the
Browns write in letters that began arriving last Tuesday.
'It would also consume a substantial part of our money,
which through our wills and through the mission work

127

of our church is destined to help many young people . . .
who may one day be able to help many more. This legacy represents the final purpose of our lives.' "*

* *The Atlanta Journal,* December 12, 1994. *Christian
  Century,* February 1–8, 1995, reports that the money
  will endow scholarships for clergy.

A Couple's Joint Suicide

Joretta L. Marshall

The art of pastoral care requires sensitivity, compassion, and a keen sense of moral integrity. Because pastoral care is part of the theological and moral activity of the church, those who would offer care must have the capacity to reflect carefully upon cases such as the one presented here, recognizing the moral complexity of the situations in which people live. Pastoral caregivers cannot afford to approach their task with either the moral rigidness that suggests there are only rights and wrongs, or with an attitude of moral laxity which may indicate that little clarity may be discerned in decision making. Instead, pastoral caregivers must be able to take a stand on issues such as suicide, recognizing at the same time that faithful persons of integrity will make choices contrary to their own perspectives. We are called to offer care to those with whom we deeply disagree, just as to those whose choices are more congruent with our moral and theological convictions.

In the case of the Browns, I would find the decision they made to be a faithful response to their situation and would not struggle with whether their decision was right or wrong. Yet, as a caregiver, I also must recognize the pain, anger, and confusion that others might experience in light of the Browns' choice to intentionally cause their own death. The opportunity for pastoral care with the Browns, their family, their church community, and the broader community is self-evident. What is less clear is the manner in which that care might be offered. The traditional functions of pastoral care—sustaining, guiding, healing, reconciling—provide a lens for offering assistance to the Browns and those who surround them. What follows is an attempt to think about pastoral care first with the Browns, and then with those who are left to make meaning of their intentional choice.

Pastoral Guidance with the Browns

Let us assume, for the moment, that the Browns are committed persons of faith who are connected to a local congregation. It is conceivable that the Browns might turn to their pastor for assistance in guiding them as they ponder their decision. Many persons would find it difficult to approach their pastoral caregiver, wondering whether that person would attempt to talk them out of their intended action, or make them feel guilty about their choice. The ability to offer care in the middle of deep disagreements must be communicated consciously by pastoral caregivers, if they are to be approached by families such as the Browns, in the process of making important, meaningful, and potentially controversial choices.

The pastoral-care function of offering guidance to the Browns in their decision making requires an examination of their motivation and reason for intentionally choosing to die. Although the Browns' specific motivations are not clear from the case study, it is possible to arrive at some hypothetical understandings that can assist the caregiver in this case.

First, the intentional choice of death reflects a belief that there are significant and meaningful ways to think about living and dying. The importance of the choices persons make about how they will die, when they will choose death over life, and how to communicate what those choices mean to family, friends, and the church community are present in the case of the Browns. In a culture that understands death as the enemy to be overcome, the attitude of the Browns feels refreshing. Here, death does not appear as the enemy, but as part of the natural rhythm of God's creation. The meaning brought to their life and death is clarified by their letters of intent distributed to their friends and colleagues. As participants in God's creative activity, it is possible to understand that the means by which persons die, or the fact that they do die, may not be as significant as the meaning they attach to that death. In this case, the meaning is related to their connection to the world around them, and their faith and trust in the future of God's activity in the world.

Second, instead of focusing on the death of the Browns in this case, it seems more appropriate to focus on the quality of the lives the Browns perceive they will experience, should they remain alive. The Browns are suggesting that the quality of their lives will diminish significantly, causing them not to experience the "abundant life" promised in the gospel. Existence in and of itself does not mark the abundance of God's promise. The quality of living is as significant as the notion that God entrusts human beings to be responsible agents in making choices about their lives. Rather than being in despair about their lives, it seems to me that the Browns are placing their faith and trust in the hope that God promises more than mere existence in life, by offering us meaningful ways to participate in our living and dying.

Third, while the constituent elements of an abundant life are often subjectively experienced, the importance of the relational aspects of life cannot be denied. The notion that the quality of one's life depends upon the quality of relationships with self, God, and others is evidenced in the Browns as they establish that part of the meaning of their death is to be found in the giving of themselves to the future and to God's activity through the church. Knowing that if their future living were to continue, they would spend most of their financial resources on prolonging life rather than living an abundant life, the Browns have chosen to be intentional about the manner in which they relate to others by offering their resources to the church.

In their intentional choice to take their lives, the Browns are not denying the relational aspects of their lives, but are building upon them in ways that suggest that they wish to "lessen the likelihood of despair and nourish the sources of hope and renewal."[1] The Browns are ultimately responsible to God and themselves for their decision, but they recognize that those around them are participants in their life and death as well. They are moving into hope by connecting with their friends through the series of letters and by outlining their commitments to the future. They are clear that the choice about their death is theirs, and that they are also responsible for participating in the interpretation of their actions to others.[2]

Fourth, the Browns have affirmed their connection to the broader community of faith of which they are a part. Choosing not to spend their financial resources on their medical treatment does not suggest that they have given up hope, nor that they have taken God's sovereignty into their own hands. Instead, it suggests that they have faithfully thought about the stewardship of their resources, as well as the nature of their relationship with God through the church. While to some it would have seemed appropriate to have spent their money to keep themselves alive, for the Browns this would have been a less responsible way of being stewards of their financial resources.

Finally, the Browns are placing their trust in the unfolding future of God's activity on earth. The money the Browns left to the mission work of the church is a faithful way to embrace the future. Here they have put their individual lives into the broader perspective of

God's ongoing activity in the world. Entrusting their financial resources to the church is not a sign of selfish grandiosity, but that they have rightfully understood that they can have an impact on the future.

Some might argue that the Browns have selfishly avoided the consequences of suffering, thereby cheating themselves of the possibility of experiencing the healing and sustaining presence of God through their suffering. While it is true that suffering often eventuates in signs of God's grace, suffering in and of itself is not redemptive. Instead, accepting the limits of their lives seems to be an appropriate response to the Browns as they seek to be part of human relatedness and community in an extended fashion. Choosing how and when one will die may offer, in this case, the possibility of expanding God's activity in the world in significant and important ways.

The pastoral function of sustaining presence might also be enacted in the life of the Browns in another way. One wonders, for example, if their pastor was available to them as they went through the process of making decisions, writing the letters, or going into the garage. Or, one wonders what images of God and what aspects of faith sustained them as they moved intentionally toward their choice of death.

The choice of the Browns to take their lives in the light of their commitments to God, to one another, to the community of faith, and to the world makes sense. Finding ways to assist them in clarifying their process, and then seeking appropriate ways to interpret their actions and responses to the broader community becomes the next focus for pastoral care.

Pastoral Care with the Community

The pastoral functions of healing, sustaining, reconciling, and guiding occur with those who are identified as the family, friends, and members of the community of faith. Questions about the meaning of death, the perplexing and competing interpretations of suicide and its moral implications, along with a host of emotional reactions, very likely will emerge in the lives of those affected by the Browns' decision. Because of the public nature of their choice, the pastoral-care functions also need to be expanded into the broader community. In working with those who are "survivors" of this suicide, it is important to remember that the perspective and reasoning of the Browns are most important to understand and communicate to others.[3] While it is impossible to understand fully that reasoning, the suggested interpretation above assists the pastoral caregiver in thinking about how to respond to those within the community who may be struggling to make sense of the choice made by the Browns.

As one author has aptly noted, "Suicide dramatically alters the life of survivors. Plans and dreams fall apart; the life story is interrupted."[4] For the Browns, for their family members, for their friends, and for their community of faith, the impact of their intentional choice to die will be felt acutely. The grieving process is complicated by the suddenness of the act and the struggles of many of us to come to terms with suicide. Finding ways to allow persons to grieve, to express their anger and hurt, their guilt or confusion, becomes one of the initial activities for the pastoral caregiver.

The need for reconciling the feelings of those who have known the Browns with the reality of their choice may emerge as one of the primary tasks. Even those who may not have known the Browns personally, but have now become responsible for the stewardship of their financial resources, will find themselves flooded with a mixture of feelings. Some will feel anger and hurt that the Browns chose to take their own lives. They may not immediately comprehend the Browns' feelings about choosing to utilize their gift of decision making to end a life, in exchange for the offering of financial resources for the ministry of God in the world. The anger may be turned into some form of blaming, reasoning that the Browns should have endured their suffering.

The pastoral caregiver at this point should not attempt to dismiss the feelings of these friends, nor should they attempt to discourage them from speaking their pain and hurt. Instead, appropriate pastoral care requires that persons be given the opportunity and encouragement to express their most profound feelings of hurt, pain, anger, and rage—at the Browns, at society, or even at God. This is what the psalmist teaches us so well in the laments. God is not afraid of hearing our angry and disheartened words. Time is required to reconcile our feelings with reality in a situation loaded with this much depth, along with the ongoing presence of pastoral caregivers in the community of faith.

The anger and pain should be not only voiced, but should be met by the compassionate response of a caregiver who offers an interpretation of the Browns and their story. If the Browns actually confided in their caregiver, it might suggest that the healing can move more progressively, as the pastoral person participates in the task of aiding persons in moving through their grief, with an assurance that the Browns made a decision that was appropriate for them. The pastor then becomes part of the interpretive frame that offers the word of response, of hope, and of courage that can be found in the story of the Browns. Again, healing from this kind of grief can be complicated and can take tremendous work on the part of those who are left to make sense of the choice to end life.

There also may be those who experience guilt about not having known that the Browns were making this choice to take their own lives. For these people, the shock of the suicide may give way to a sense of guilt about not having intervened in some way. One of the important realities in this case is that the choice to die was in the hands of the Browns, not in the hands of persons around them. The Browns seem to have come to their decision by thinking clearly and carefully about their life situation, and then responding in a way that was appropriate and reasonable to them. Hence, those within the community who may carry guilt need, once again, the compassionate presence of a pastoral caregiver who can remind them that the choice belongs to the Browns, not to the community.

Offering guidance to those who experience the guilt or burden of responsibility for making decisions about the financial resources left by the Browns also may become a task for those who would offer care. Assisting these persons in thinking clearly about the intentions of the Browns makes possible the movement from guilt and anxiety toward hopeful trust.

An important responsibility for pastoral caregivers in the aftermath of this particular intentional death is to think about the responsibility of the society, and of the church, to those who are aging or who suffer with incurable diseases. We corporately share the responsibility, in many ways, for the choices the Browns felt compelled to make. The medical culture of which we are part knows more about prolonging life than about assisting persons in making faithful and meaningful choices in response to illness. A prophetic response of the pastoral caregiver is to challenge the church, the community of faith, and the society, to think carefully about our public health-care system, and the way it forces people to make these kinds of choices.

Pastoral care with the Browns, their family, their friends, their community of faith, and the broader society of which they are a part requires persons who can remain steadfast in the face of controversial and competing claims about what it means to be faithful. I support the Browns' choice and find in it a faithful response to a complex situation. Similarly, I would pray for those of us who remain, to continue to reflect upon the emerging meaning offered to us by the living and dying of the Browns.

NOTES

1. Dana Wilbanks, "Ethical Perspectives in Review," *Perspectives on Suicide*, ed. James T. Clemons (Louisville: Westminster/John Knox Press, 1990), p. 72. In this article Wilbanks offers various perspectives about suicide. The notion of relational ethics builds, in part, upon the arguments put forth by the work of James Gustafson.
2. Ibid., p. 66.
3. Ibid., p. 67.
4. Richard D. Parsons, "Suicide Survivors: Intervention—Preventions—Postvention," *Clinical Handbook of Pastoral Counseling, Volume 2*, ed. Robert J. Wicks and Richard D. Parsons (New York: Paulist Press, 1993), p. 648.

A Couple's Joint Suicide

J. Philip Wogaman

Taking the High Road?

Every pastor, from time to time, has to agonize over the suffering of terminally ill people who can look forward to nothing but pain. I remember one man who had a form of cancer that was particularly painful. In the midst of his suffering, he spoke to me about how such a physical crisis is also a spiritual crisis.

"Phil," he said, "I look out and see nothingness. There is no answer from across the void." What can one say to that? One can try to be a friend and hope that will be an expression of the love of God that is deeper than words. All of us can agree on that, even though we generally fall short of being that kind of deep support to others. But what about the further steps suggested by this account of a joint suicide? What are we to say about actions to end it all? Euthanasia? Suicide? Assisted suicide?

The pastor in this report plainly believes that the couple, Richard and Helen Brown, have taken "the high road to death." Forgoing treatment, they believe, will enable them to leave a sizable legacy for good charitable purposes. It seems to have worked out that way, with $10 million being left to United Church of Christ charitable organizations. On the face of it, this gift of money is generous; perhaps it is already doing much good.

Questioning the Assumptions

I do not stand in judgment. But there are two important but unspoken assumptions in the story. The first is that decent treatment for the Browns would, in fact, consume their fortune. No doubt that is true, if both of their medical-care programs were pursued with maximum aggressiveness. But are there not numbers of arthritic or asthmatic patients receiving care for much less money? Does an Alzheimer's patient need to receive such expensive care? We may not know for sure, although we do know that there is an important distinction between withholding maximum treatment and actively causing death through euthanasia or suicide. I wonder whether in this case there might have been a middle-ground option that would have preserved both the Browns' lives and the bulk of their fortune.

The other assumption is more important: It is, or seems to be, that the Browns had come at last to the point where their lives were no longer worth living. In the case of the Alzheimer's condition, one can, I suppose, conceive of a final state in which the brain is almost totally vacant. Is that true here? If so, Helen Brown was not a knowing participant in her own death. If she was not a conscious actor in this act of suicide, was this a more or less benign form of murder? The account is not quite clear at that point. We may assume that she was aware of her condition and fearful of its final outcome. In the case of her husband, are we to conclude that his life was so afflicted by arthritis and asthma to have become essentially useless, no longer worth the cost of staying alive?

"Intrinsic" Versus "Instrumental" Values

This is a hard case because we are asked to balance the inherent value of their lives, to themselves and to others, with the instrumental value of whatever $10 million can buy. Philosophers distinguish between "intrinsic" value and "instrumental" value. Something that is "intrinsically" good is good for its own sake. An "instrumental" value, on the other hand, is good only because it helps to gain or preserve the intrinsic good.

Life itself is an intrinsic good; money is instrumental. Maybe the $10 million has been put to use saving the lives of others. Perhaps it is contributing to the inherent value of the lives of those who otherwise would have a wretched existence.

But can we weigh and measure this in such a utilitarian way? If so, would we then begin to put a price tag on the value of life of all sorts of physically challenged people, concluding that the money used to help them would go much further if put to other charitable purposes? I do not want to make this sound easy. Society often must choose an instrumental good over an intrinsic one—for the sake of even greater intrinsic goods. A major engineering project, like a dam or a highway system, is likely to cost several lives in accidents, but in the end, other important values will be served. Medical service itself often involves such tradeoffs as decisions are made in the allocation of scarce resources. But we must always keep the distinction between the "intrinsic" and the "instrumental" clearly in view.

Suffering Can Serve Compassionate Ends

The Browns case does not refer to serious physical suffering, though Richard Brown doubtless experienced real pain through his arthritis and asthma. By coincidence, my mother-in-law had both those conditions, lived into her mid-eighties, and died one night after a severe asthmatic attack that probably triggered a heart attack. I'd have to say that her life, right to the end, was of enormous value, both to herself and to a wide circle of friends. Perhaps Richard Brown suffered more, or feared that he would, particularly if he were not to receive very expensive treatment.

Even so, would you say that physical suffering in itself justifies suicide or assisted suicide? Maybe so.

Some argue that we are more compassionate in our treatment of dumb animals than of human beings. Beyond a certain point, we put a dog or a horse out of its misery. Why not human beings?

No doubt we should be more compassionate and humble as we face such a question. And yet, there is another side. For human beings, perhaps unlike dogs or horses, suffering itself can serve compassionate ends. Those words can slip across the tongue too cheaply, if people have not faced the agony for themselves. But I have known people who suffered a long time and ministered all the while to those around them—glad, in the end, that there had been no shortcuts taken. The man referred to at the beginning of this article ultimately received his answer "from across the void," and I shall never forget the communion service that several of us celebrated with him shortly before his death, and the individual "blessing" he conferred upon each of us. His life had great value, even in the midst of that awful disease; he came to see that and to celebrate it.

Nor can I forget a terminally ill woman of the church I serve. She was dying of cancer and, by a curious turn of fate, was herself an oncological nurse—meaning that she dealt with cancer patients all the time and understood the pain she would suffer all too well. She carefully rationed out her own dosages of pain-relieving morphine so she could stay in alert mental contact with her loved ones until the end. For her, the meaning of life was not to be found in the presence or absence of pain.

The Higher Calling of Ethics: Affirming Life

In citing these stories, I could also note other, less heroic souls. None of us knows how we ourselves would respond to such challenges until we actually face them. Still, is it not the higher calling of ethics to affirm life as we believe it *ought* to be? One does not have to condemn those who have taken, or who contemplate taking the Browns' way out. But should we not encourage one another to "stay the course" as long as natural life is given to us? Here the distinction between the active taking of life and the withholding of heroic medical measures can be important. Modern medicine creates more situations in which a decision to withdraw support is wise and humane. When, in a clearly terminal case, a decision is made no longer to pursue treatment aggressively, there are (and ought to be more) good hospices, in which a patient's last days can be made more comfortable and meaningful, at lower cost than the usual intensive care unit of a modern hospital.

Thus far we have considered the Browns' case as a matter of personal moral decision making—their own and those who might assist them. My leaning in such cases is toward the continued affirmation of life, despite pain, despite what might appear an undignified existence, despite the loss of many of the physical and mental capacities one has previously enjoyed. As a matter of personal moral decision making, I would place the "burden of proof" against suicide or euthanasia, reserving such extreme measures for exceptionally rare situations. Faced with that in my own life, I frankly do not know how I would react, or whether this intellectual conclusion could bear the weight of protracted personal pain or loss. I do know that I have been in pastoral situations in which personal meaning and loving relationship continued despite enormous pain and loss. Again, that is to see this as a matter of personal moral decision making.

Social and Legal Implications

What about the social and legal implications? Should attempted suicide, or at least assisted suicide, be penalized? Should such things be treated as criminal acts? I am less prepared to say yes to that. I am still struggling with that question, because I know that pain can be almost unbearable and that it can be unrelieved by any hope, short of death, of its ending. And yet, I don't want the medical profession ever to drift lightly into this. This is a real moral dilemma, not an imaginary one with a case to be made on both sides. De facto, I suspect, the medical profession is accorded a certain latitude, but with a rigorous legal system remaining in place to assure that the exception does not drift into being the rule. Perhaps, in time, we will come to accept more explicitly the forms of pain reduction that also shorten life. I am not sure we are ready yet to ease the legal tension too much.

But more must be said. We are one of the few advanced societies in which the cost of medical care is treated as personal cost more than social cost. The Browns did not want to have their life savings eaten up by expensive health care. Granted that they could have spent all $10 million on the very best doctors, hospitals, and so on, did they have the real option of modest terminal care at much lower cost? Early in this essay, I implied that such an option might have existed. Now I must acknowledge that I am not certain that it did. But if it did not, is that not an indictment of the way we organize health-care delivery in this country? In other countries, decisions must sometimes be made to allocate resources away from expensive treatment in what are likely to be hopeless cases. The Browns would not have objected to that. But in countries with better systems for universal health-care delivery, there also is often a better hospice system to make terminal patients more comfortable. Can we respond to a case like the Browns' without recognizing our own responsibility as a nation, to assure universal health-care delivery and provide a really good hospice system?

The Meaning of Life

The social responsibility cuts even deeper than that. Lurking between the lines in this story, I sense the poignancy of loss of meaning in life. To be sure, the Browns' act is a meaningful gift, seen on one level. Their suicide made it possible for a large sum of money to go toward worthwhile social causes. But what kind of "signal" were they receiving from this culture, that their lives were no longer worth $10 million (or whatever amount of money would be yielded by their giving up their lives)? Excluding the factor of pain, were people somehow conveying to them that an arthritic asthmatic or an Alzheimer's victim are no longer to be valued? Nothing is said in this published account about "death with dignity," but there may be a hint here that people so afflicted have lost their human dignity—or at least that the only way to preserve human dignity is to go out in one decisive act.

If I have correctly caught the hint, does this mean that there was a risk that they would have lost the *respect* of others? If so, we all may need to reassess the basis on which we accord respect to other people. Ultimately, we are dealing here with theological issues. Theologically, respect is grounded in God's assessment of our lives. Physical limitations and disabilities are not understood, in Christian theology, as signs of God's disfavor or disrespect, any more than physical prowess or attractiveness is the basis of our real worth.

A similar point can be made about physical suffering. The meaning of life, for Christians, does not ride on the pleasure/pain principle. To Christians, in fact, the deepest symbol we have of human meaning is also a symbol of suffering. The cross, in fact, is also our deepest symbol of redemption through suffering.

Measured against the reality of suffering, these words

are awfully cheap. I acknowledge that. Yet, contained
within the deep mystery of our existence, is there
not more than a glimmering of truth to the notion that
we are called to share the burdens, not try to escape
them?

STUDY GUIDE

Responding to the joint suicide of a couple who left a $10 million fortune to the church, two distinct perspectives are shared.

Joretta L. Marshall believes the couple's action was a faithful Christian response to their situation and their estimate of a future diminished life. She affirms their evaluation that simply existing is not to be equated with the "abundant life" promised in the Gospel. She probes psychological dimensions faced by the couple, as well as by family and friends who are left after a suicide. The couple's decision not to expend their financial resources simply to prolong their lives was not an act of despair, but of hope, as demonstrated by their investing in God's future mission activity through the church.

The moral appropriateness of the decision is challenged by J. Philip Wogaman. Wogaman places the "burden of proof" against suicide and euthanasia, reserving such extreme measures "for exceptionally rare situations." He suggests a "middle-ground option" that would have provided treatment and care to the couple without expending their fortune. He asks about informed consent—was the woman with Alzheimer's "a knowing participant in her own death?" Utilitarian philosophies that put a price tag on the value of life must be avoided. "Life itself is an intrinsic good; money is instrumental." He explores the public-policy ethics of universal health care and a good hospice system, as well as Christian understandings of pain and suffering.

Items for Reflection

1. Should the church and other charities discourage actions like the Browns'? Share your concerns and reasoning.

2. Marshall suggests that many persons would find it difficult to approach a clergyperson to discuss the possibility of suicide, fearing disapproval. How would you feel about approaching your clergy?

3. Marshall emphasizes her concern for those left behind after a life-terminating act. What experiences have you had with persons who have "survived" the suicide of a loved one?

4. Wogaman suggests that sometimes "suffering itself can serve compassionate ends." Have you known persons such as those he describes, persons who have ministered to others through their suffering?

5. Do you feel that a human being is obligated to bear whatever suffering is brought by chronic or terminal illness, never taking steps to end his or her life?

CHAPTER SEVEN

When It's My Turn,
How Shall I Decide?

Donald E. Messer

For everything there is a season, and a time for
every matter under heaven:
a time to be born, and a time to die.

Ecclesiastes 3:1-2

Though my father's formal education ended at the
eighth grade, he taught me both how to live and how to
die. The son of immigrant parents from Norway and
Germany, Dad worked hard and lived simply, first as a
South Dakota farmer and then as a small-town busi-
nessman. A man of few words, he seldom spoke, but his
Christian values of care, compassion, and love toward
his family and his community were clearly self-evident.

Without warning, my father was diagnosed with
incurable liver cancer. Three weeks later, he died. Just
as he had quietly taught his family how to live, he spent
his final days demonstrating to us how to die. His
instructions were clear: No expensive life-prolonging,
but ultimately futile treatments like chemotherapy. No
heroic actions. Bring the family home from around the
country, so love and hugs and kisses could be
exchanged. Take care of mother. No intravenous feeding, once the family could no longer care for him at
home and he would have to return to the hospital.

Death for Dad came swiftly, and he departed this life

with dignity and grace. A few days later, family and
friends gathered in our small prairie-town church and
sang:

> Soar we now where Christ has led, Alleluia!
> Following our exalted Head, Alleluia!
> Made like him, like him we rise, Alleluia!
> Ours the cross, the grave, the skies, Alleluia![1]

Decision Making's Most Personal Level: To Live or Die

People realize that death often snatches away life, and
no choices are permitted. At other times, options exist,
so when it is my turn, how shall I decide? Will I accept
my destiny with simple clarity and conviction as my
father did, or will I struggle to live beyond my allotted
days? Will I be free to make my own decisions, or will I
be forced by legal systems, hospital authorities, or other
circumstances to die the way they determine acceptable? How will I live out my Christian faith in the face
of death?

These questions perplex not only this author, but
probably every person who contemplates the sunset
moments of his or her own life. This chapter attempts
to create an ethical framework to assist in thinking
through one's principles and consequences, when a
choice exists to prolong or terminate one's own life. It
seeks to examine both right-making and wrong-making
characteristics of decision making as they relate to the
issues of refusal/withdrawal of treatment, physician-
assisted termination of life, suicide and assisted suicide.
A complex series of moral and ethical questions that
must be addressed are reviewed. In doing so, a high
degree of complexity and ambiguity inherent at every
point in the process is recognized.

Even the language we choose reflects this complexity

and ambiguity. We cannot completely escape the pejorative power of the words we use. Suicide, for example, is an emotionally charged term which historically has been associated with sin and crime. Thus to speak of "assisted suicide" tends to connote something quite different from talking of "assisted death."[2] Public discussion in the press and journals tends to use the phrase "assisted suicide," which corresponds more closely to the position of those who traditionally oppose the idea, rather than employing the term "assisted death," which advocates of change might prefer.

For most Christians the questions under discussion are not matters simply decided, but tug at the deepest emotional, ethical, and theological tissues of our being. These are not merely theoretical queries, but existential dilemmas that potentially face us all. Many other ethical challenges, such as abortion, genetic engineering, participation in war, and so on, may or may not directly impact a person, but none of us can escape confronting the final days of our own lives or those of our loved ones.

This chapter does not pretend to offer a formula for enacting public policy, but rather focuses on the realm of personal decision making at what must be the most personal level of choice imaginable—to live or to die. Unless choice is restricted or denied by circumstances of health or economics, or by others, then all of us have a degree of freedom for making this decision. We may choose to surrender this liberty to medical personnel, family, legal systems, or religious authorities, or we may prefer to exercise our personal autonomy and seek to control the final dance of death. This author does not prescribe to others how they should act, since each person before God must decide his or her own final fate. Rather, I offer an ethical framework that seeks to enable individuals to be conscientiously faithful to their basic theological convictions and moral commitments, as well as empower them to discover a fitting response to their given situation.[3]

As Christians, we want to be true to our theological ethics, while being realistic and responsible in discovering an appropriate response to a given situation. We struggle to make correct decisions because we are a caring and compassionate people who worship a loving God. Whether we are thinking about ourselves or have a role in determining the fate of another, we are caught in a complex of conflicting claims and variant values.

"Playing God" with Life and Death

Christians have always protested against "playing God" when it came to decisions of life and death. Our inclination has been to let "nature" take its course— "God gives and God takes away." But the revolution in medical science now means that human beings are already and inevitably "playing God," so we are forced to make more conscientious decisions. In the past, when medical technology was more limited, the extension of life was generally circumscribed by time, but now the possibility of prolonging existence has been significantly expanded. Thus questions about "the quality of life" have become more and more problematic. These fears are expressed in a paraphrase of the Twenty-third Psalm:

> Medical science is my shepherd;
> I shall not want,
> It maketh me to lie down in hospital beds;
> It leadeth me beside the marvels of technology.
> It restoreth my brain waves;
> It maintains me in a persistent vegetative state for its
>   name's sake.
> Yea, though I walk through the valley of the shadow of
>   death,

I will find no end to life;
Thy respirator and heart machine they sustain me.
Thou preparest intravenous feeding for me
In the presence of irreversible disability;
Thou anointest my head with oil;
My cup runneth on and on and on and on.
Surely coma and unconsciousness shall follow me all the
     days of my continued breathing;
And I will dwell in the intensive care unit forever.[4]

Lest this paraphrase be dismissed as an individual's exaggerated fears, it should be noted that a recent ten-year study of 9,105 patients in five hospitals nationwide discovered a large percentage of people subjected to aggressive and dehumanizing medical treatments they did not want. The researchers revealed in the *Journal of the American Medical Association* that roughly half of the seriously ill patients in the study endured "prolonged dying," suffered acute pain, were hooked to medical machinery, and often were attended by a physician largely ignorant of or inattentive to their wishes. The treatment for the average patient who died cost nearly $100,000, and one-third of their families report losing most or all of their savings in the process.[5] *People are experiencing intensive care, instead of intensive caring.*

Biblical Perspectives Regarding Suicide

Christians characteristically turn to the Bible when seeking counsel for God's will in their lives. In regard to issues of suicide, however, neither the Old nor the New Testament offers clear and compelling testimony. As Pope John Paul II candidly acknowledged in his encyclical *Evangelium Vitae,* the issue, as such, is never mentioned in the Bible.[6] Analysis of the six direct accounts of suicide recorded in the Hebrew Bible (Abimelech, Samson, Saul and his armor-bearer, Ahithophel, and

Zimri), and the one direct report (Judas) in the New Testament, demonstrate no specific approval or condemnation of suicide.[7] Prior to Augustine (A.D. 354–430), there exists little or no evidence of Christian condemnation of suicide; in fact, suicidal practice may have been quite common among Christians.

Indirectly, however, scriptural texts often have been used since Augustine. Most influential has been the interpretation of the commandment "you shall not murder,"[8] first enunciated by Augustine as a prohibition against suicide. Other texts (NRSV) often cited against euthanasia include Job 1:21 ("the Lord gave, and the Lord has taken away"), I Corinthians 6:19 ("your body is a temple of the Holy Spirit"), and Ephesians 5:29 ("For no one hates his own body, but he nourishes and tenderly cares for it"). On the other side, Christians have pointed to Jesus' choice of death on a cross and the calls to martyrdom and self-sacrifice (Mark 8:34-35, John 13:37, I John 3:16, Romans 5:7) as justification for considering hastening death and even suicide.

Biblical proof-texting provides no quick answers to the issues posed by this book. Christians thus must engage in theological and ethical reflection, drawing not only on scriptural insights, but also on historical traditions, human experience, and standards of reason.[9]

To aid in our decision making, I have sought to diagram an ethical edifice in which our decisions will emerge. Like all visual attempts to express complicated theoretical ideas, it has its limitations, but hopefully it will help us to keep in mind some of the central considerations involved. In Table One I have outlined some of the basic Christian convictions and ethical commitments required for faithful allegiance to basic principles. Table Two delineates factors involved in finding a fitting or appropriate response to a given situation. The two are combined in Table Three, indicating that ultimately, an individual decision often must be made within a web of competing and conflicting values and factors. It is never a matter of simple computer analysis, but of conscientious reflection and action.

Being Faithful to Basic Principles

Responsible Christians seek to live out their theological convictions and ethical commitments in their decision-making. Table One illustrates these overlapping theological convictions and ethical commitments.

TABLE ONE

Theological Convictions	Ethical Commitments
1. God as Giver of life	1. Truth telling
2. Human Autonomy	2. Do good and prevent evil
3. Law of love	3. Do no harm
FAITHFUL ALLEGIANCE TO BASIC PRINCIPLES	

Three key theological convictions, among many others, persistently emerge in the debate over euthanasia and assisted suicide: God as the Giver of life, human autonomy or self-determination, and the law of love. Likewise, three ethical commitments play a primary role in Christian decision making on this subject: truth telling, beneficence, and nonmalfeasance. Obviously, others can and should be added, but for illustrative purposes, these six central principles will be examined.

God as the Giver of life is a fundamental Christian concept, affirming the divine Creator's role in human life. A human being is not the absolute owner of one's own life, but is dependent upon God's loving grace. The gift of life is derived from God, not from society. Persons are created in God's image and are expected to protect, not destroy life. Because God is the Giver of life, human life is viewed as sacred and inviolable, not to be sacrificed to society's interests.

Historically, Christians have believed that it was a denial of God's loving providence to assert that life no longer has quality or purpose. Contemporary Christians have argued that medical technology now can reduce people to a persistent vegetative state, and when a person is only biologically alive, the very humanness that made life sacred is gone.

Pope John Paul II proclaims that "the sacredness of life gives rise to its inviolability," therefore characterizing suicide as "a gravely immoral act" and euthanasia as "a grave violation of the law of God."[10] On the other hand, an understanding of a loving and merciful Creator prompts other Christians to believe that hastening death in the face of intractable pain and suffering, or other limited circumstances, can be profoundly moral and even the will of God.

In the classic Christian view, death is not the end of life. Life does not precede birth (as it does in doctrines of reincarnation), but life does succeed death. Thus, to end one's "life" in the vernacular and secular sense, is not to end one's "life" in the Christian sense of the term.

Human autonomy, or self-determination, characterizes the distinctive quality of personhood. Persons are not made to be puppets dangling on the strings of a creator God. Rather, they are endowed with the freedom and obligation to make decisions—to be responsible for self, society, and creation. Blind obedience to preordained laws or authorities is not expected, but rather that persons will seek to discern the will of God in every situation and respond in faithful and loving action. Called to live in the world, persons are expected to use their intellect and reason to make reflective judgments and decisions.

A biblical model of human autonomy or self-determination is portrayed in Genesis (Gen. 2:18-20). God calls upon Adam to "name the animals" and waits to see what Adam will call them. As Hebrew biblical scholars have noted, to "name" something is not simply to label it; it is to give it a meaning and order it in the nature of things. Hence, Adam is called upon to continue the creation by bringing order into being, rather than simply replicating preordained orders.[11]

Proponents of assisted death or suicide emphasize self-determination or choice, while opponents emphasize the limits of autonomy. Advocates argue that people want to govern or control their own lives, not be ruled by the judgment of others. Without limits on liberty, say the opposing side, the floodgates are open to euthanasia.[12]

The 1992 Supreme Court ruling in *Planned Parenthood v. Casey* illustrates this debate. In this abortion case, the Court decided that the right to privacy was an explicit right, rooted in the Fourteenth Amendment. The majority declared that "at the heart of liberty is the right to define one's own concept of existence, of meaning, of the universe, and of the mystery of human life." Dissenting Justice Antonin Scalia warned that this expansive definition of liberty could encompass "homosexual sodomy, polygamy, adult incest, and suicide." When the Ninth Circuit Court of Appeals in 1996 upheld an individual's right to decide "how and when to die," it appealed to the Fourteenth Amendment's guarantee of personal liberty. Judge Stephen Reinhardt wrote for the 8 to 3 majority that "a competent, terminally ill adult, having lived nearly the full measure of his life, has a strong liberty interest in choosing a dignified and humane death, rather than being reduced at the end of his existence to a childlike state of helplessness, diapered, sedated, incompetent."[13]

The law of love describes the Christian standard of behavior for all human relationships. It also reflects the very "agape," self-giving love of a merciful God. The Great Commandment enunciated by Jesus was to love God with heart, soul, mind, and strength, and to love one's neighbor as oneself. This norm applies not only to motives and intentions, but also is to be sought in terms of means and ends. Compassion and caring are cardinal values to be embodied in terms of both principles and consequences. It is not sufficient simply to say that we are acting "rightly and leaving the results with the Lord." This norm calls us to attempt to create loving consequences by doing the most merciful act possible.

Critics of physician-assisted suicide label such acts not mercy, but murder. Love never justifies homicide. Yet other Christians insist that if you truly love another, you will respect that person's wishes to be free from disabling pain or meaningless existence. Love may prompt us to terminate our own lives or advocate assisted death for loved ones.

Truth telling is a moral maxim rooted in the Hebrew Bible ("You shall not bear false witness" [Exodus 20:16, NRSV]), and in the New Testament witness of Jesus Christ as the "Truth," meaning that God was revealing in Christ the very essence of the divine. Ideally, the church is called to be a moral community of both truth seekers and truth tellers. Certainly in circumstances regarding medical health and well-being, truth seeking and telling is imperative. Irreparable harm can be done by deliberate false or partial diagnosis and information.

Lying is a wrong-making characteristic, for truth telling is at the very heart of human relationships. To tell a "white lie" or "fudge the truth" robs the patient of a fundamental right to know the truth and to act accordingly.[14] Informed consent for accepting or refusing treatment, and for determining whether one wants to terminate one's life, necessitates having the most complete diagnosis and information available.

Beneficence, or benefiting ourselves or others by doing good or preventing evil, permeates Christian theology and ethics. Ironically, this impulse toward altruism is reflected both by those who would champion the alleviation of suffering by assisted suicide, and by those who would restrict its possibility because they fear a "slippery slope," moving from abortion to assisted suicide to euthanasia to mercy killing to exterminating "undesirable" people. Beneficence demands respect and action in favor of the rights and dignity of persons. Yet too often, academic debates that focus on passive or active euthanasia obscure the particular painful predicament of the person. "To love your neighbor as yourself" means that the best interests and welfare of suffering persons assert priority.

The principle of beneficence clearly manifests itself in the hospice movement. Dedicated to the relief of pain and suffering, hospice personnel are known for their merciful care of patients and patients' families. At their best, Christian hospitals and hospices aim, in Lisa Sowle Cahill's words, "to be in solidarity with those who suffer." Historically, these agencies have opposed participating in physician-assisted suicide, as being contrary to their understanding of Christian beneficence. Some, however, are now asking whether beneficence, as the prevention of evil, does not justify participation in some limited forms of assisted death.

Do no harm or nonmalfeasance (the responsibility not to injure or harm others) often is held to be the most stringent right-making characteristic. Versions of "you shall not murder" (Exodus 20:13, NRSV) permeate most theological traditions. The principle that suicide and euthanasia in any form are always morally wrong has been bedrock to Christian thinking since Augustine, and has deeply influenced the development of secular law in Western cultures. Theologically, it stems from beliefs which emphasize that only God, the Giver of life, should determine life's termination, that killing (of oneself or another) is always immoral.

The physicians' Hippocratic Oath declares: "I will give no deadly medicine to anyone if asked, nor suggest any such counsel." In medical ethics, the categorical imperative is "first, do no harm." However, to encourage healing and avoid greater suffering and death, doctors do preventive surgery, which entails a degree of hurt and harm, and runs risks of fatal consequences. Yet there is a vast moral difference between intentional and unintentional action, even though the consequences can be strikingly similar.

In seeking to be faithful to these six basic theological and ethical principles, Christians of good conscience and goodwill may reach differing conclusions, since often these values are in conflict or cannot all be simultaneously realized. Prayerful meditation and reflection must precede careful action.

Finding an Appropriate Response to a Given Situation

Therefore, Christians seek to be both responsible and realistic when facing issues of euthanasia and suicide. The authors in this book, while differing dramatically in perspectives and approaches, have acknowledged these dimensions as they addressed the nuances of particular cases. Table Two outlines these criteria: determining facts, fixing moral limits, calculating consequences, being good stewards, moving beyond absolutes, and living with "dirty hands."

Finding appropriate or fitting responses presumes the possibility of more than one course of action, thus presenting decision making not as a simple mathematical equation of adding and subtracting, but of dividing questions by reflection and understanding multiple consequences.[15] Each of the cases described in this book represents individuals who sought to find fitting responses to the critical situations they experienced. Presumably, each struggled to do what she or he deemed good and right. Not being in their "shoes," we (and the contributing authors) have the liberty of "second-guessing" their choices, free from the perplexities of their pain and the ambiguities and anxieties of their decisions.

TABLE TWO

FITTING RESPONSE TO A GIVEN SITUATION	
Seeking to Be Realistic	**Seeking to Be Responsible**
1. Determining facts	1. Being good stewards
2. Fixing moral limits	2. Moving beyond absolutes
3. Calculating consequences	3. Living with "dirty hands"

The determining of facts cannot be overemphasized. The quality of one's ethical judgments often stems from the accuracy of information gained and the perceptions one possesses. What facts and factors have been considered or ignored? What medical alternatives exist to the contemplated action of euthanasia or suicide? Social science teaches that what persons define as real becomes real in terms of consequences.[16] The irreversiblity of death makes an ethical imperative out of determining the facts. At some point, of course, a decision must be made. As theologian Robert McAfee Brown notes, "Don't wait until all the facts are in before you act. The facts are never all in."[17]

Fact-finding is not always precise and can prove problematic. A survey of physicians in Oregon, published in the *New England Journal of Medicine,* demonstrated the difficulties they would encounter if an enacted assisted-suicide law in their state were to go into effect. The law permits physicians to prescribe lethal doses of medication to terminally ill, mentally incompetent adults with less than six months to live. Another physician must confirm the diagnosis and the patient's mental competence. However, half the doctors said they were not confident that they could predict when a patient would have less than six months to live. A fourth were unsure they could tell when a patient was clinically depressed. Half expressed uncertainty about what drugs they should prescribe to a patient who wanted to die, and also what would happen if their prescriptions failed to hasten death and only did further harm to the patient.

Fixing moral limits is essential for the conscientious Christian. By recognizing ambiguity and the necessity of going beyond absolutism to deal with exceptions in unusual circumstances, we are in danger of ending up with a position of "anything goes."

The ethical person says that there are limits beyond which one may not go. Draw a line, and shout "No," because to go beyond this borderline would be to violate and undermine all the good one seeks to achieve. For me, such lines include, first, an insistence that no person should be forced to suffer pain that is persistent or progressive. Second, in order for persons to make informed choices, they need to be made aware of options and opportunities for treatment, including appropropriate medications for pain and depression. Third, decisions for treatment or hastening death should be based upon informed and voluntary consent, including advanced directives and/or expressed intentions to family, friends, and/or physician. Fourth, review and approval by a medical-ethics oversight panel (in a reasonably speedy time frame) should be required before physician-assisted death occurs. Fifth, prohibition of government-sponsored euthanasia of those who may be deemed "burdensome" to society (e.g., persons who are of the indigent poor, or have mental and physical disabilities, or are elderly and incapacitated) must be enacted and enforced. Sixth, the rights for assisted life or assisted death must be protected by careful medical and legal procedures for those for whom informed consent proves impossible (underage or senile and other types of "incompetent" patients). The burden of ethical and legal proof would be upon those who transgress these six precepts.

Calculating consequences and weighing risks must be approached with a degree of humility and prudence, since we never can be sure that the good intended will actually happen or that unintended evil or harm may not result from even the best of intentions and actions. In ethics, the principle of proportionality suggests that the good achieved must outweigh the evil done. This does not mean some 51/49 percentage split of good over evil, but rather that there should be an overwhelming preponderance of good achieved, with a minimum amount of evil experienced.

Calculating the consequences of life and death involves many dimensions and should not be considered

lightly. Fear of the abuse of euthanasia or assisted suicide, however, should not automatically prohibit termi-
nally-ill persons from being released from their unnecessary suffering. Policy makers must guard against abusive
evil, but not become paralyzed by inaction, thereby failing to make caring and compassionate alternatives possible, such as making available proved but prohibited
medication, and even assisted death.

One way of attempting to calculate consequences is
to provide advance directives as to what one expects
one's physician, hospital, and family to do in a life-
threatening situation. Shocking studies have demonstrated that without living wills, courts have honored
men's previously expressed preferences regarding the
withdrawal of treatment some 75 percent of the time,
but have honored women's preferences only 14 percent.[18] By preparing living wills, do-not-resuscitate
orders, and durable powers of attorney, one can seek to
control one's own destiny in the final days of life. Unfortunately, some evidence indicates that these sometimes
go unheeded, and a wave of lawsuits is now seeking to
hold hospitals, nursing homes, and doctors liable, saying
that treatment given against a patient's will is a form of
assault and battery.[19] To help avoid such situations, persons are encouraged to share their advance directives
with their family, doctors, and others.

Being good stewards of life's resources poses a perplexing dimension for Christians. Ethicists correctly
warn about the dangers of placing a price tag on the
value of life. The poor and disenfranchised minorities
are particularly vulnerable. Already in the United
States, they have limited access to good health care (40
million people, 75 percent of the population under 65,
are not covered by health insurance).[20] Unrestrained
euthanasia would inevitably have a disproportionate
impact on their communities. The lessons of the Holo-

caust must not be forgotten.[21] Coercive pressures from family members and others eager for an inheritance do occur and serve as a chilling reminder of the need for rigid guidelines and strict safeguards.

Yet Christians cannot ignore questions of economics, if they are to be faithful stewards of the resources God has entrusted to them. Though my father never mentioned the cost of his hospital care, I have always suspected that he didn't want to prolong his life needlessly, in part because he wanted to preserve for my mother their very limited life savings. When he died, her Social Security check was reduced significantly. It is a tragic misuse of money to expend it needlessly in futile treatments.

How sad and scandalous to learn that one-third of all families whose loved one died after aggressive intensive-care procedures reported losing most or all of their savings! Further, theologian John B. Cobb, Jr., has noted that "the vast expenditure on the elderly to keep us alive, often against our wishes, exhausts public resources that are not then available for public health services for pregnant mothers and young children." Former Colorado Governor Richard D. Lamm confirms Cobb's insights:

> America spends almost eight times as many public funds on those over 65 as on those under 65. We spend 15 times as many public funds on the elderly as on children—despite the fact that children are much more likely to be poor. America has the highest rate of life expectancy for 80 year olds in the world, but we are 20th in infant mortality. We pay, through Medicare, the health bills of millionaires, but we forget to vaccinate kids. Six hundred thousand millionaires get a social security check every month (and thus are eligible for Medicare), while 600,000 women gave birth last year with little or no prenatal care. Few would say this was a just distribution of limited health resources.[22]

Moving beyond absolutes means that no ethic, however well-intentioned or seemingly good, can be automatically applied as an absolute without taking into consideration the particular facts and factors involved in a given situation. Truth is not always crystal clear, and human beings struggle to discern the will of God. Moving beyond absolutes does not, however, mean abandoning ethical norms that provide basic direction and guidance. It does not mean becoming radically relativistic or drastically situational, making decisions solely case by case, with no undergirding theological or ethical framework. Rather, it acknowledges that ethical norms can be "overwhelmed by extreme circumstances," while at the same time other norms can be "underwhelmed" by trivial application.[23] To allow for justifiable instances of euthanasia and suicide does not mean endorsing unlimited and uncontrolled forms of both.

Unconditional obedience to absolutist ethical mandates proves to be neither invariably good nor inevitably right. One can imagine a given situation when loyalty to such commitments would lead to an absurd situation (for example, answering the query of a rapist by truthfully identifying a loved one). On the other hand, to abandon all basic principles is to wander into a total relativistic and situational world, with no restaints against evil.

A Christian ethic of responsibility bridges the two extremes of absolutism and relativism by an approach which asserts that certain right- and wrong-making characteristics or principles can be identified, defended, and applied in decision making.[24]

Living with "dirty hands" is a phrase borrowed from political ethics, referring to the great anguish one experiences in an imperfect world when one is forced to choose between lesser evils. Being involved in "necessary evil," such as helping a patient or parent terminate his or her own life inflicts scars on one's soul. Though I knew what my father wanted, and I was convinced he was right, it still hurts when I think about telling the doctor not to provide intravenous feeding. Had I not done what he requested, I also would have had to bear feelings of guilt. Requesting medical professionals and family members to assist in death forces them into ethical and legal quandaries, in which they must have the right to say "No."

Yet what the public wants is not medical doctors (like Jack Kevorkian) who sometimes seem too enthusiastic in participating in physician-assisted suicide, but rather competent and merciful persons who only reluctantly in extreme cases do the morally disagreeable.[25] Though the 300,000-member American Medical Association firmly opposes physician-assisted suicide, recent opinion polls in the United States indicate that up to 75 percent of the public favor doctors helping terminaly-ill patients die.[26] The Eleventh International Conference on AIDS in Vancouver, Canada, reported that medical doctors surveyed in the United States, Canada, England, and the Netherlands have prescribed deadly doses of narcotics to assist persons who seek "self-deliverance" from their pain and suffering.[27]

A recent controversial survey published in the *New England Journal of Medicine* suggests that one out of five intensive-care nurses has deliberately hastened patients' deaths. They are not self-appointed "angels of death," but these medical practitioners either acted on their own, or with at least the tacit consent of doctors or families. They didn't view themselves as self-appointed "angels of death," but as nurses full of anxieties and questions, as they sought to determine where palliative care ends and euthanasia begins. Though the survey has been challenged as being flawed, it does demonstrate the "dirty hands" dilemma increasingly faced by persons in the medical profession.[28]

Making a Personal Decision

Sorting through this matrix of theological and ethical convictions in order to determine an appropriate personal decision never proves simple. Inevitably, we are torn between competing claims and conflicting values. In pondering a given action, I must always weigh both the right-making and wrong-making characteristics inherent within a particular decision, and then decide which is likely to be more right than wrong. This personal element of decision making can be excruciatingly difficult, since absolute certainty is rarely obtainable.

The characteristics may be clear as charted in Table Three, but a person does not instinctively or automatically know which element should have greater weight. Right-making characteristics are guides to action, but not guarantees of right choice.[29] It is not always possible to uphold every moral or theological norm, even though we desire to do so.

Overall, individual judgment must rely on what is determined as a preponderance of good, or perhaps the minimum of evil, in a particular situation. If I am a medical doctor facing a terminally ill patient, I must ask whether by giving more medication to alleviate pain, I am not hastening death by adding excess strain to the heart. But would not the relief of suffering represent a preponderance of good, even though a degree of malevolence is involved? If I am a family member, what, if any, are the limits of love? If my loved one begs me to terminate his or her life—and I know his or her painful predicament—can I refuse to be of assistance, even though I know the potential legal consequences?

If it is I who desires the termination of my own life, due to persistent and inescapable pain, or the foreseeable consequences of a stroke, Alzheimer's disease, or AIDS, do I dare risk taking my own life? What if I fail and simply make matters worse for myself and my loved ones? What if I succeed, but in such a way as to create permanent psychological scars for my family? Is it ever appropriate to ask another person to break the law and assist me in escaping my earthly hell? No easy answers exist, but the questions must be addressed by conscientious Christians contemplating suicide or assisted death in any form.

The dilemma of decision making means examining all known alternatives, exploring possible consequences, and exercising intellectual discipline and imaginative empathy in a given situation. Ultimately, however, a person's decision will be made in light of conscience and character. Sometimes he or she will make a choice that under other circumstances would be forbidden, but in this particular case seems best, when weighing available alternatives. Though one may select this course of action—as a doctor, family member, or for oneself—one may still refrain from generalizing or universalizing it. One may realize that under other conditions, another value or action may be preferable, so one hesitates to make it a binding rule in all cases.

The ambiguities of life and death and the complexities of Christian ethics finally reach resolution in the crux of each person's conscience and character. The quality of a decision rests with the decision-maker. Individual decision making, however, has never been accepted as a sole arbiter of morals, by either Roman Catholics or Protestants. Consultation with others in the community always has been a prescribed corrective to guard against a solipsism that would so highly individualize decision making as to discard the insights, experience, and expertise of family, friends, and the broader community. Christians seek to act with consideration, not only of themselves, but of the consequences to family and society.

Religious rules and governmental laws help establish moral boundaries. They point to what is usually deemed right and wrong, good and evil. These are not absolute for all time, but approximations of what other persons have conscientiously thought to be good and right and fitting. Yet they deserve careful and prayerful consideration in our decision making, lest we claim to know too much and fail to learn from others. We should *begin* with respect for the laws of the land, presuming they reflect the dominant cultural, political, and moral values of the culture. Thus Robert Bolt, in *A Man for All Seasons*, has Sir Thomas More declare:

> The law, Roper, the law. I know what's legal not what's right. And I'll stick to what's legal. . . . I'm *not* God. The currents and eddies of right and wrong, which you find such plain sailing, I can't navigate, I'm no voyager. But in the thickets of the law, oh, there I'm a forester. . . . What would you do? Cut a great road through the law to get after the Devil? . . . And when the last law was down, and the Devil turned round on you—where would you hide, Roper, the laws all being flat? This country's planted thick with laws from coast to coast—man's laws, not God's—and if you cut them down, d'you really think you could stand upright in the winds that would blow then? Yes, I'd give the Devil benefit of law, for my own safety's sake.[30]

Christian ethics, however, do not end with due regard for religious rules and governmental laws, since both can reflect group prejudice and represent repressive actions, as witnessed by centuries of racial, gender, and sexual orientation discrimination. At prophetic moments, they need to be challenged and changed.

Unfortunately, a gap almost always exists between ethical norms and contextual reality, particularly in complex cases such as the one this book has been

TABLE THREE

Theological Convictions	Ethical Commitments
1. God as Giver of life	1. Truth telling
2. Human self-determination	2. Do good and prevent evil
3. Law of love	3. Do no harm

FAITHFUL ALLEGIANCE TO BASIC PRINCIPLES

Individual Conscience

DECISION

Individual Action

FITTING RESPONSE TO A GIVEN SITUATION

Seeking to Be Realistic	Seeking to Be Responsible
1. Determining facts	1. Being good stewards
2. Fixing moral limits	2. Moving beyond absolutes
3. Calculating consequences	3. Living with "dirty hands"

exploring, and which individual readers may be contemplating. The dilemma of decision making, however, forces us to make choices and take actions.

Christians are not immune from mistakes. In certain instances, to hasten to terminate life may be the right thing to do, but probably much less often than might first appear. The moral burdens of ethical responsibility—of making proper decisions, of choosing between lesser evils, of facing severe criticism or legal consequences, and even of doing things that one would prefer not to do—all weigh heavily on the soul of a conscientious person. Trusting in God's forgiveness and grace, we move forward, wishing we knew precisely what God wills for us in life and death. Therefore, let us bear in mind the unusual axiom of Martin Luther to "sin strongly." Or, to put it in another way, do our best and pray for forgiveness!

A Personal Word

Personally, I am neither eager to die nor do I fear death. As a Christian, I believe in the Resurrection and life beyond. Whatever else heaven is, I hope I can play Chinese checkers with my Grandma and rummy with my Dad!

What I want is to leave this life without causing undue pain or suffering for my loved ones. I see no reason to have my life prolonged by machines and unnecessary medical procedures. I have no desire to be a burden, economically or personally, to others. I plan to live out my life to the fullest, but when I have exhausted all energy and intelligent living, then I trust God will provide a means for departing this world. I will have talked to my loved ones and left advance directives via a living will and powers of attorney. If my organs and tissues are of any value, I will gladly donate them so that others might live. Whatever financial resources I may have can be better spent by my survivors and the charities I designate, than by having them consumed by expensive caretaking industries.

When it's my turn, how shall I decide? Of course, none of us knows, but I pray that when faced with life versus death choices, I will have an opportunity to think through the issues theologically and ethically, and be free to make a responsible choice in light of my Christian faith.

NOTES

1. Charles Wesley, "Christ the Lord Is Risen Today," *The United Methodist Hymnal* (Nashville: The United Methodist Publishing House, 1989), verse 4, p. 302.
2. Helping me to understand this distinction was an unpublished and untitled scholarly document by Marv Miller, Dakota Wesleyan University, May 1996.
3. This chapter draws upon and adapts the ethical theory developed in my book *Christian Ethics and Political Action* (Valley Forge, Penna.: Judson Press, 1984). For more detailed discussion of the theory, see especially pp. 79-148.
4. "Psalm for Today," by an anonymous Unitarian minister, *Hemlock Quarterly*, April 1989, cited by Richard D. Lamm in "The Brave New World of Health Care," *The 21st Century Series*, The Center for Public Policy and Contemporary Issues, University of Denver, June 1993.
5. See *Journal of the American Medical Association*, November 1995. Reported in the *San Francisco Examiner*, November 23, 1995, and in *The Honolulu Advertiser*, November 22, 1995.
6. Kenneth L. Woodward, "Life, Death and the Pope," *Newsweek*, April 10, 1995.
7. James T. Clemons, "Suicide, The Bible, and Ethics in Contemporary American Society," *Occasional Papers*, January 20, 1987, pp. 6-8. See also Clemson, *What Does The Bible Say About Suicide?*

(Minneapolis: Augsburg Fortress Press, 1990). Note Abimelech (Judg. 9:50-57), Samson (Judg. 16:21-31), Saul and his armor-bearer (I Sam. 32:1-13), Ahithopehl (II Sam. 17:23), Zimri (I Kings 16:15-20), and Judas (Matt. 27:3-5). Jonah (Jonah 1:12) might be viewed as an "attempted" suicide; see Elie Wiesel, *Five Biblical Portraits* (Notre Dame: University of Notre Dame Press, 1981).

8. Exod. 20:13 and Deut. 5:17 NRSV.

9. Two main types of ethics—deontological and teleological—especially have influenced Christians over the centuries. In the preceding chapters, both types of ethical arguments have been advanced. Different authors in this book have given greater weight or consideration to one or the other style of argument.

Deontological theories insist that certain actions are right or wrong, regardless of their consequences. Empirical circumstances ultimately don't make any difference; what is crucial is faithful allegiance to basic principles. What is right and what is wrong? Consequences, intentional or unintentional, are basically unimportant; what is imperative is that one have the proper attitude, motivation, or principle in mind. The ends never justify the means.

Theological theories focus on the consequences of actions. Ends can sometimes justify the means. Consequences do make a difference. What is the highest good? Sometimes this is expressed in the utilitarian notion of "the greatest good for the greatest number." Other times, it is more personal, believing that if the good and well-being of another can be advanced, even by unusual or even usually repugnant means, then the action is ethical.

10. John Paul II, Encyclical, *Evangelium Vitae* ("The Gospel of Life"), 1995, No. 40, 64, and 65.

11. See Delwin Brown, *To Set at Liberty: Christian Faith and Human Freedom* (Maryknoll, N.Y.: Orbis Books, 1981), pp. 9, 15, 35, 53.

12. See Charles Colson and Nancy Pearcey, "Lady with a Blue Dress On," *Christianity Today*, June 17, 1996, p. 72, and Charles Colson, "Casey Strikes Out," *Christianity Today*, October 3, 1994, p. 104. Allen Verhey, "Choosing Death: The Ethics of Assisted Suicide," *Christian Century*, July 17-24, 1996, p. 719, foresees a potential boomerang effect to overemphasizing human autonomy:

    Providing the choice of assisted suicide to the vulnerable, to the dependent, to those who are no longer in control, is recommended, doubtlessly, as a way to increase their options, to enable them to assert their autonomy and to take control. Maximizing freedom in this way expresses a culture that values autonomy, independence, and control. But it also forms both attitudes toward the suffering and the attitudes of those suffering. The effect of maximizing freedom in this way may be to make it more difficult for the sick and suffering—the dependent, those whose lives seem out of control— to refuse the option of death, harder to justify their existence.

13. See Tamar Lewin, "Ruling Sharpens Debate on 'Right to Die'," *The New York Times*, March 8, 1996. This ruling struck down a Washington state law that made assisted suicide a felony. It also increased the probability that the Oregon state law allowing physician-assisted suicide would be permitted to go into effect. Two months later, a unanimous decision by the 2nd Circuit Court of Appeals in New York struck down portions of a state ban on assisted suicide, on the basis of the 14th Amendment. An appeal of these cases and a

ruling by the United States Supreme Court is expected. The last time the Supreme Court spoke directly on this subject was in the 1990 Nancy Cruzan case, when it declared that under the 14th Amendment, patients had a constitutional right to refuse unwanted medical treatment.

14. The burden of proof must be on the person who endorses the right to die. The ethical presumption rests with truth telling. Even the devils themselves, said Samuel Johnson, do not tell lies to one another, for the society of hell could not exist without the structure of truth!

15. H. Richard Niebuhr, in *The Responsible Self: An Essay in Christian Moral Philosophy* (New York: Harper & Row, 1963), p. 147, characterized an ethic of responsibility from other approaches in this way:

Responsibility, however, proceeds in every moment of decision and choice to inquire: "What is going on?" If we use value terms, then the differences among the three approaches may be indicated by the terms, the *good,* the *right,* and the *fitting;* for teleology is concerned always with the highest good to which it subordinates the right; consistent deontology is concerned with the right, no matter what may happen to our goods; but for the ethics of responsibility, the *fitting* action, the one that fits into a total interaction as response and as anticipation of further response, is alone conducive to the good and alone is right.

16. W. I. Thomas said, "If men define situations as real, they are real in their consequences," quoted in Robert K. Merton, *Social Theory and Social Structure,* rev. ed. (New York: The Free Press, 1957), p. 421.

17. Robert McAfee Brown, "The Experiences of the '60s: A Few Lessons," *Christian Century,* January 3-10, 1979, p. 7.

18. S. Miles and A. August, "Court, Gender, and the 'Right to Die'," *Law, Medicine and Health Care,* January-February, 1990.

19. Tamar Lewin, " 'Wrongful Life' Suits Filed," *The Denver Post,* June 2, 1996. A jury in Michigan awarded $16.5 million to Brenda Young, her mother, and her daughter, because a hospital failed to follow her signed advance directives four years ago. Young, now age 38, is incapacitated and requires total care. Lewin reports, "She must be fed, bathed, diapered and, at night, tied into bed so she does not push herself over the padded bedrails. Sometimes she manages a few intelligible words: 'Water' or 'Bury me.' But mostly she screams, over and over."

20. Spencer Rich, "No Rest for the Uninsured," *The Washington Post National Weekly Edition,* May 13-19, 1996.

21. How these lessons themselves are appropriated may, however, be subject to debate. For example, news photos from Australia in 1996 portrayed protesters demonstrating against the world's first law in their Northern Territory that allows voluntary euthanasia. Their placards replaced "euthanasia" with "euthanazia."

22. See Richard D. Lamm, "The Brave New World of Health Care," *The 21st Century Series,* The Center for Public Policy and Contemporary Issues, University of Denver, 1993, p. 8.

23. Charles Fried, *Right and Wrong* (Cambridge, Mass.: Harvard University Press, 1978), p. 12.

24. This approach corresponds with that developed by W. D. Ross in *The Right and the Good* (Oxford: Clarendon press, 1930) and Arthur J. Dyck in *On Human Care: An Introduction to Ethics* (Nashville: Abingdon Press, 1977). See also

W. D. Ross, *Foundations of Ethics* (Oxford: Oxford University Press, 1939). Other right-making characteristics, or *"prima facie"* duties, include promise keeping, reparation, and gratitude. Note Messer, *Christian Ethics and Political Action*, pp. 123-44.

25. See Bernard Williams, "Politics and Moral Character," in *Public and Private Morality*, ed. Stuart Hampshire (London: Cambridge University Press, 1978), p. 64.

26. See Carol J. Castaneda, "Agonizing Over the Right to Die," June 7, 1996, for results of a *USA Today*/CNN/Gallup Poll in April, 1996. The percentage has climbed from 65% favorable in 1990 and 53% in 1973. In June 1996, the American Medical Association reaffirmed for the fourth time in the past two years its long-held stand against euthanasia and assisted suicide.

27. Daniel Q. Haney, "Many Doctors Willing to Assist AIDS Suicides," *The Denver Post*, July 11, 1996: 53% of the doctors in a San Francisco-area group of AIDS specialists admitted writing prescriptions for narcotic overdoses.

28. Gina Kolata, "Nurses in Survey Admit Helping Patients Die," *The Denver Post*, May 23, 1996, and Ann Schrader, "Survey on Hastening Death Assailed," *The Denver Post*, May 24, 1996.

29. Sissela Bok reminds us in *Lying: Moral Choice in Public Life* (New York: Pantheon Books, 1978), pp. 77-78, that establishing rules among moral principles cannot be done in the abstract, but always emerges in the concrete:

Similarly, while it is obscure to claim that weight and length conflict in the abstract, there are concrete cases where both cannot be satisfied, where you cannot get a thing the length you want and the weight you want, as where you need fifteen yards of heavy chain, but have only the strength to carry home five pounds of it. In the same way, you cannot always make a choice, or expect others to make it, which achieves both the fairness and the beneficence you desire. Moral principles, just like length and weight, represent different dimensions by which we structure experience and can therefore present conflicts in concrete cases but never in the abstract. It is for this reason that the search for priority rules among moral principles in the abstract is doomed to fail; one might as well search for such privacy rules among pounds, yards, and hours in the abstract.

30. Robert Bolt, *A Man for All Seasons* (New York: Random House, 1960), pp. 37-38.

STUDY GUIDE

Since death and dying are not human options, but inevitable existential realities to be faced by every person, Christians are called to think through these issues theologicaly and ethically.

The pejorative power of words is acknowledged, since terms like suicide and euthanasia are emotionally charged due to historic association with sin and crime. Thus to speak of "assisted suicide" tends to connote something quite different from "assisted death."

Due to medical technology's ability to prolong life significantly, coeditor Donald E. Messer contends that we are already "playing God," and thus often are forced to make choices about when to hasten or end life.

Basically, the Bible offers no specific approval or condemnation of suicide. Beginning with Augustine (A.D. 354-430), Christian teachings have condemned suicide. In contemporary times, however, many Christians have challenged this absolutist approach.

Messer offers an ethical framework to help guide persons in thinking through their decisions and actions. Seeking to be faithful to basic principles, Christians will struggle to affirm overlapping theological convictions (God as Giver of life, human self-determination, the law of love) and ethical commitments (truth-telling, doing no harm, doing good/preventing evil). Wanting also to find an appropriate response to their given situation, Christians aim to be both realistic (determine facts, fix moral limits, and calculate consequences) and responsible (be good stewards, move beyond absolutes, and live with "dirty hands").

Identifying characteristics of right and wrong, however, does not automatically guarantee right choice. After consultation with family and others, each person must conscientiously make his or her own difficult and agonizing decisions.

Items for Reflection

1. Since language tends to have negative or positive connotations and thus affects us emotionally, explore how the use of words makes a difference in the way we think and feel about subjects such as "assisted suicide" or "assisted death."
2. Discuss the biblical and theological teachings regarding terminating one's own life or assisting another to do so.
3. Share with others the personal experiences you may have had when someone you loved was experiencing a prolonged death. Describe the person, illness, prognosis, quality of life, family support, and decisions that were required. Indicate what emotional, theological, and ethical factors played a role in the decision-making process. In retrospect, what could have made the situation "better" for your loved one and others?
4. Since death is not a human option, review with others the steps that a person might take now to ensure more control in the dying process. Enter into dialogue about what you pray will happen at that critical stage in your life.

BIBLIOGRAPHY

Created for Concerned Laity and Clergy

The selections annotated here were chosen for readability and relevance to commonly asked questions. The list is intentionally brief and intended for busy people who want a few excellent resources. It merely touches the surface of available materials. For those who wish to pursue the subject in greater depth, the citations listed here, particularly the periodicals, are a good place to start.

BOOKS

Beauchamp, Tom L., and Robert M. Veatch, editors. *Ethical Issues in Death and Dying,* 2nd ed. Upper Saddle River, N.J.: Prentice Hall, 1996. For readers who desire a single volume comprehensive commentary on current issues related to the ethics of death and dying, this book is an excellent resource. Topics such as "Problems in Law and Public Policy," "Problems in the Morality of Physicians' Actions," and "Decisions on Behalf of Children and Formerly Competent Adults" are discussed by authors representing a number of involved professions. Each section ends with a suggested-readings list.

Berger, Arthur S., and Berger, Joyce, editors. *To Die or Not to Die? Cross-disciplinary, Cultural and Legal Perspectives on the Right to Choose Death.* New York: Praeger, 1990. The selections included here are from a variety of religious and cultural perspectives: Jewish, Islamic, African, Japanese, Indian, and European. Useful appendixes include policy statements from inflential groups, a digest of U.S. judicial decisions relating to the right to refuse life-prolonging treatment, and a table of states that have living-will statutes.

Callahan, Daniel. *What Kind of Life: The Limits of Medical Progress.* New York: Simon & Schuster, 1990. Callahan believes our health-care problem is greater than it appears on the surface, not just a matter of improved financing, equity, and efficiency. Perhaps it is a crisis about the meaning and nature of health. We have come to desire what we no longer can have in unlimited measure—a healthier extended life.

Clemons, James T. *What Does the Bible Say about Suicide?* Minneapolis: Augsburg Fortress, 1990. Using clear language, Clemons offers comment on every biblical reference to suicide and attempted suicide in the Bible, noting that the references describe different situations, rather than one static category. None of the references condemns the act. The section on the historical development of the church's theological position against suicide is particularly helpful.

Cobb, John B. *Matters of Life and Death.* Louisville: Westminster- John Knox Press, 1991. Chapter 2, "The Right to Die." In a four-chapter paperback, Cobb responds to his own concern that too many theologians shy away from the most difficult and controversial issues of their day. He provides a thoughtful analysis of suicide and assisted suicide. A good study book for church groups.

Deciding About Life's End: A United Methodsit Resource Book About Advance Directives. Dayton, Ohio: Health and Welfare Ministries Program Dept.,

General Board of Global Ministries, The United
Methodist Church, and The United Methodist Association of Health and Welfare Ministries, 1994. This
short paperback booklet begins with definitions and
ethical commentary on the two most common procedures used to prolong life—cardiopulmonary resuscitation and artificical feeding. It includes a Choice in
Dying resource list of inexpensive pamphlets on such
topics as "Pain Management" and "Making Life-Support Decisions." The appendixes from this booklet are
used with permission as the appendixes to this book.
The glossary of terms is excellent. A great resource
for local churches.

Early, Kevin E. *Religion and Suicide in the African-
American Community*. Westport, Conn.: Greenwood
Press, 1992. What began as a sociological dissertation
under the title "It's a White Thing," has been expanded into a book. In the U.S.A., the suicide rate for
whites is about twice as high as the rate for blacks.
Early's research into African-American perspectives
on suicide does not include material related specifically to terminal illness. He concludes that strong
condemnation by the black church is a significant factor in keeping the suicide rate low in black communities, and also suggests that strong family and community ties still buffer blacks against hopelessness or
"giving up."

Hamel, Ron P., editor. *Choosing Death: Active Euthanasia, Religion and the Public Debate*. Park Ridge Center for the Study of Health, Faith, and Ethics.
Philadelphia: Trinity Press International, 1991. Short,
readable, and full of useful information. The chapter
by Martin Marty and Ron Hamel, "Some Questions
and Answers," offers clear and succinct answers to
frequently asked questions. Other chapter titles
include "A Brief Historical Perspective," "Views of

the Major Faith Traditions," "Is Active Euthanasia Justifiable?" (with comments by six ethicists), and "Should We Have a Public Policy?"

Hauerwas, Stanley. *Naming the Silences: God, Medicine, and the Problem of Suffering.* Grand Rapids: William B. Eerdmans, 1990. Hauerwas, reframing the common question, "Why does God allow suffering?" asks instead, "Why does that question, particularly as it relates to illness, seem so important to us?" Using stories of dying children, he seeks to help Christians understand how God can use suffering as a way to assist believers in discovering the true meaning of hope and love.

Hilton, Bruce. *First Do No Harm: Wrestling with the New Medicine's Life and Death Dilemmas.* Nashville: Abingdon Press, 1991; Leader's Guide, 1994. Hilton's easy-to-grasp style and format make this book ideal for individuals and study groups. It covers a number of bioethical dilemmas, including life-support systems, durable power of attorney, and euthanasia.

Humphry, Derek. *Final Exit.* The Hemlock Society, P.O. Box 11830, Eugene, Oregon 97440. Distributed by Carol Publishing, Secaucus, New Jersey, 1991. This controversial book offers detailed explanations of the ways a patient may end his or her own life, with or without assistance from others.

John Paul II. "Evangelium Vitae: The Gospel of Life, Eleventh Encyclical, March 25, 1995," *The Pope Speaks,* July/August 1995, pp. 199-281. The authoritative Roman Catholic statement condemning euthanasia and suicide in all forms.

Melton, Gordon. *Euthanasia, Official Statements from Religious Bodies and Ecumenical Organizations.* Detroit: Gale Research Inc., 1991. A comprehensive collection of official statements by religious bodies, including Buddhists, Jehovah's Witness, Independent Fundamental Churches of America, Church of Christ, Scientist, as well as Roman Catholic, Eastern Orthodox and Protestant statements. Good reference book.

Quill, Timothy E. *Death and Dignity: Making Choices and Taking Charge.* New York: W. W. Horton & Co. 1993. This book is dedicated to Diane, the patient Quill assisted in death. Written after her death, Quill expresses the hope that the pain her family endured after her case was made public will, ultimately, lead to better public understanding and a more humane public policy. He discusses the Hippocratic Oath and the limitations of comfort care, offering a wider range of options for the dying (including those who are mentally incapacitated).

PERIODICALS

Periodicals are the best sources for short, up-to-date commentary on moral and ethical thinking about euthanasia, assisted suicide, and suicide. The journals noted below represent the best of both conservative and liberal perspectives. Articles by most of the contributors in this book can be found in one or more of them. Most of these are accessible at public libraries or through interlibrary loan.

Periodicals from Ethics Centers

Hastings Center Report, the bimonthly publication of The Hastings Center, a nonprofit, nonpartisan organization that carries out education and research programs on ethical issues in medicine, the life sciences, and the professions. The Hastings Center, 225 Elm Road, Briarcliff Manor, NY 10510. Daniel Callahan, editor.

Hastings Center Report, A Special Supplement, January/February, 1989, titled "Mercy, Murder, and Morality: Perspectives on Euthanasia," was compiled to help people think through the theological, philosophical, professional, and policy issues presented by the issue of euthanasia.

A later special supplement of the *Hastings Center Report* (volume 21, 1991) was titled "Practicing the PSDA" (Patient Self-Determination Act). This federal law raised a host of ethical and pragmatic issues for health-care providers and their patients. Written by noted scholars, articles in this special supplement addressed concerns for implementing provisions of the act to make advance directives work for both patients and the institutions that serve them.

Making the Rounds in Health, Faith, and Ethics. In 1995, this newsletter replaced a more comprehensive journal, *Second Opinion,* as the semimonthly publication of the Park Ridge Center for the Study of Health, Faith, and Ethics, 211 E. Ontario, Suite 8900, Chicago, IL 60611. Martin E. Marty, senior editor.

Religious News Journals

The Christian Century, a weekly ecumenical publication edited by James M. Wall, a United Methodist clergyman. The Christian Century Foundation, 407 S. Dearborn St., Chicago IL 60605.

Christianity Today is a monthly evangelical publication edited by George K. Brushaber, a Baptist clergyman. Christianity Today, Inc., 465 Gundersen Drive, Carol Stream IL 60188.

Commonweal, a Roman Catholic biweekly, reviews issues of public affairs, religion, literature, and the arts. It is edited by Margaret O'Brien Steinfels. Commonweal Foundation, 15 Dutch St., New York NY 10038.

First Things is a conservative monthly journal of Religion and Public Life, an interreligious institute whose purpose is to advance religiously informed public philosophy for the ordering of society. Richard John Neuhaus is editor-in-chief. First Things, P.O. Box 3000, Dept. FT, Denville NJ 07834.

The Other Side: Where Justice and Peace Embrace; Where Faith and Love Join Hands is a liberal evangelical bimonthly periodical edited by Mark Olson. Order by calling 1-800-700-9280. Address: 300 W. Apsley St., Philadelphia PA 19144.

Sojourners, a liberal evangelical monthly publication edited by Jim Wallis, offers a progressive Christian voice with an alternative vision for both church and society. Sojourners, 2401 15th St. NW, Washington DC 20009.

APPENDIX A

This is a generic form. Please check with officials in your state or with your attorney for the form appropriate to your individual needs.

Appointment of a Health-Care Representative

Patient name: _____

I hereby appoint _____ _____

                                             Relationship to Patient
                                             (relative, friend, etc.)

Address: _____

Home Telephone: _____ Work Telephone: _____

as my representative to act in my behalf in all matters concerning my health care, including but not limited to providing consent or refusing to provide consent to medical care, surgery, and/or placement in health-care facilities, including extended-care facilities. This appointment shall become effective at which time and from time to time as my attending physician determines that I am incapable of consenting to my health care.

I hereby give the following instructions to my representative (optional):

1. _____

_____

_____

2. _____

_____

_____

I authorize all health-care providers to rely upon consents and authorizations provided by my representative. I hereby ratify all that my said representative shall do by virtue of this appointment. I agree to be financially responsible for health-care services performed in reliance upon consents executed by my health-care representative.

_____ Date: _____
Patient Signature

_____ Date: _____
Adult, other than representative

APPENDIX B

This is a generic form. Please check with officials in your state or with your attorney for the form appropriate to your individual needs.

Living Will Declaration

Declaration made this _____ day of _____ (month, year).

I, _____, being at least eighteen (18) years old and of sound mind, willfully and voluntarily make known my desire that my dying shall not be artificially prolonged under the circumstances set forth below, and I declare:

If at any time I have an incurable injury, disease, or illness certified in writing to be a terminal condition by my attending physician, and my attending physician has determined that my death will occur within a short period of time, and the use of life-prolonging procedures would serve only to prolong the dying process artificially, I direct that such procedures be withheld or withdrawn.

(Indicate your choice below before signing this declaration.)

_____ including artificially supplied nutrition and hydration,
_____ except that artificially supplied nutrition and hydration are be continued, and that I be permitted to die naturally, with only the performance or provision of any medical procedure or medication necessary to provide me with comfort care or to alleviate pain.

In the absence of my ability to give directions regarding the use of life-prolonging procedures, it is my intention that this declaration be honored by my family and physician as the final expression of my legal right to refuse medical or surgical treatment and accept the consequences of the refusal.

I understand the full import of this declaration.

Signed _____ ⟋ Date _____

_____

City, County, and State of Residence

The declarant has been personally known to me and I believe (him/her) to be of sound mind. I did not sign the declarant's signature above for or at the direction of the declarant. I am not a parent, spouse, or child of the declarant. I am not entitled to any part of the declarant's estate or directly financially responsible for the declarant medical care. I am competent and at least eighteen (18) years old.

Witness _____ Date _____

Witness _____ Date _____

APPENDIX C

This is a generic form. Please check with officials in your state or with your attorney for the form appropriate to your individual needs.

Life-Prolonging Procedures Declaration

Declaration made this ____ day of _____ (month, year.)

I, _____, being at least eighteen (18) years old and of sound mind, willfully and voluntarily make known my desire that if at any time I have an incurable injury, disease, or illness determined to be a terminal condition, I request the use of life-prolonging procedures that would extend my life. This includes appropriate nutrition and hydration, the administration of medication, and the performance of all other medical procedures necessary to extend my life, to provide comfort care, or to alleviate pain.

In the absence of my ability to give directions regarding the use of life-prolonging procedures, it is my intention that this declaration be honored by my family and physician as the final expression of my legal right to request medical or surgical treatment and accept the consequences of the request.

I understand the full import of this declaration.

Signed _____ Date _____

_____
City, County, and State of Residence

The declarant has been personally known to me and I believe (him/her) to be of sound mind. I am competent and at least eighteen (18) years old.

Witness _____Date _____

Witness _____Date _____

APPENDIX D

This is a generic form. Please check with officials in your state or with your attorney for the form appropriate to your individual needs.

Organ/Tissue Donation

In the hope that I may help others, I hereby make this anatomical gift, if medically acceptable, to take effect upon my death. The words and marks below indicate my desires.

I give: (a) _____ any needed organs or tissue

(b) _____ my body for anatomical study if needed (medical research or education)
(c) only the following organs or tissue:

_____

_____

_____

★ ★

Signed by the donor and the following witnesses in the presence of one another:

_____   _____

Signature of Donor   Date of Birth of Donor

_____   _____

Dated signed   City and State

_____   _____

Witness   Witness

APPENDIX E

This is a generic form. Please check with officials in your state or with your attorney for the form appropriate to your individual needs. This form is not a legal document, but indicates your wishes when you cannot decide.

ADVANCE MEDICAL DIRECTIVE
WORKSHEET

I, _____, MAKE THIS MEDICAL DIREC-
TIVE AS AN INDICATION OF MY WISHES REGARDING
MEDICAL TREATMENT IN THE EVENT THAT ILLNESS
SHOULD MAKE ME UNABLE TO COMMUNICATE THEM
DIRECTLY. I MAKE THIS DIRECTIVE, BEING 18 YEARS
OF AGE OR MORE, OF SOUND MIND, AND APPRECIAT-
ING THE CONSEQUENCES OF MY DECISIONS.

Signature	Date	Witness to Signature	Date

LEGEND:

W = *I want*   **WT** = *I want a trial:*
DNW = *I do not want*   *If no clear improvement,*
UND = *I am undecided*   *stop treatment*

1. **CARDIOPULMONARY RESUSCITATION (CPR)**—The use of drugs, artificial breathing, and electric shock to start the heart beating.
2. **MECHANICAL BREATHING**—breathing by a machine through a tube inserted into the airway.
3. **ARTIFICIAL NUTRITION AND HYDRATION**—nutrition and fluid given through a tube in the veins, nose, or stomach.
4. **MAJOR SURGERY**—(such as removing part of the intestines) with potential complications and discomfort.
5. **KIDNEY DIALYSIS**—cleaning the blood by machine or by fluid passed through the abdomen.
6. **CHEMOTHERAPY**—drugs used to fight cancer.
7. **MINOR SURGERY/INVASIVE DIAGNOSTIC TESTS**—(such as removing some tissue or using a flexible tube to

look into the stomach) with potential complications and discomfort.
   8. **BLOOD OR BLOOD PRODUCTS**
   9. **ANTIBIOTICS**—drugs to fight bacterial infection.
  10. **SIMPLE DIAGNOSTIC TESTS**—tests with little potential for complications and discomfort, such as blood tests or x-rays.
  11. **PAIN MEDICATIONS**—even if they dull consciousness and may indirectly hasten my death.
  12. **OTHER INSTRUCTIONS** _____

SITUATION A—If I become acutely ill and unable to express my wishes and in the opinion of my physicians *there is reasonable hope that I can return to my previous state of health,* then my wishes regarding the use of the following, if considered medically reasonable, would be (appropriate boxes marked): **W   DNW   UND   WT**

1) ☐ ☐ ☐ ☐   7) ☐ ☐ ☐ ☐

2) ☐ ☐ ☐ ☐   8) ☐ ☐ ☐ ☐

3) ☐ ☐ ☐ ☐   9) ☐ ☐ ☐ ☐

4) ☐ ☐ ☐ ☐   10) ☐ ☐ ☐ ☐

5) ☐ ☐ ☐ ☐   11) ☐ ☐ ☐ ☐

6) ☐ ☐ ☐ ☐

SITUATION B—If I become acutely ill and unable to express my wishes and in the opinion of my physicians *there is little or no realistic hope that I will recover from my illness and that death is likely to be within a short period of time regardless of what is done,* then my wishes regarding the use of the following, if considered medically reasonable, would be (appropriate boxes marked): **W   DNW   UND   WT**

1) ☐ ☐ ☐ ☐   7) ☐ ☐ ☐ ☐

2) ☐ ☐ ☐ ☐   8) ☐ ☐ ☐ ☐

3) ☐ ☐ ☐ ☐   9) ☐ ☐ ☐ ☐

4) ☐ ☐ ☐ ☐   10) ☐ ☐ ☐ ☐

5) ☐ ☐ ☐ ☐   11) ☐ ☐ ☐ ☐

6) ☐ ☐ ☐ ☐

SITUATION C—If I become acutely ill and unable to express my wishes and in the opinion of my physicians *I have severe permanent brain damage which would make me unable to recognize people or make rational decisions, and from which there is no expected recovery (i.e., persistent vegetative state),* then my wishes regarding the use of the following, if considered medically reasonable, would be (appropriate boxes marked): **W DNW UND WT**

1) ☐ ☐ ☐ ☐   7) ☐ ☐ ☐ ☐

2) ☐ ☐ ☐ ☐   8) ☐ ☐ ☐ ☐

3) ☐ ☐ ☐ ☐   9) ☐ ☐ ☐ ☐

4) ☐ ☐ ☐ ☐   10) ☐ ☐ ☐ ☐

5) ☐ ☐ ☐ ☐   11) ☐ ☐ ☐ ☐

6) ☐ ☐ ☐ ☐

I have reviewed this document with the patient.
Signature _____, M.D. Date _____

INDEX